Joni
Eareckson Tada

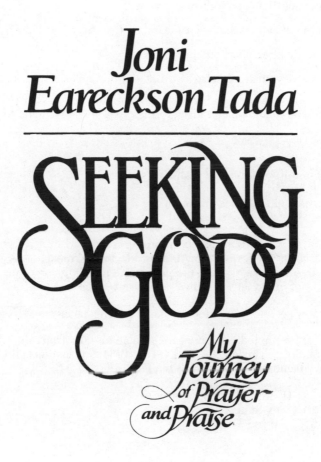

SEEKING
GOD

My
Journey
of Prayer
and Praise

Wolgemuth & Hyatt, Publishers, Inc.
Brentwood, Tennessee

The mission of Wolgemuth & Hyatt, Publishers, Inc. is to publish and distribute books that lead individuals toward:

- A personal faith in the one true God: Father, Son, and Holy Spirit;

- A lifestyle of practical discipleship; and

- A worldview that is consistent with the historic, Christian faith.

Moreover, the Company endeavors to accomplish this mission at a reasonable profit and in a manner which glorifies God and serves His Kingdom.

This book was produced with the assistance of The Livingstone Corporation.

Unless otherwise noted, all Scripture quotations are from the Holy Bible, New International Version. © 1973, 1978, 1984 International Bible Society. Used by permission of Zondervan Bible Publishers.

Wolgemuth & Hyatt, Publishers, Inc.
1749 Mallory Lane, Suite 110
Brentwood, Tennessee 37027

Library of Congress Cataloging-in-Publication Data

Tada, Joni Eareckson.
    Seeking God : my journey of prayer and praise / Joni Eareckson
Tada.
        p. cm.
    ISBN 1-56121-086-2
    1. Spiritual life. 2. God. 3. Prayer. 4. Praise of God.
5. Tada, Joni Eareckson. I. Title.
BV4501.2.T215 1990
248.8'6—dc20   91-3899
                                                                    CIP

Help Me To Pray

O God, early in the morning I cry to you.
Help me to pray,
and to concentrate my thoughts on you:
I cannot do this alone.

In me there is darkness,
But with you there is light;
I am lonely,
but you do not leave me;
I am feeble in heart,
but with you there is help;
I am restless,
but with you there is peace.
In me there is bitterness,
but with you there is patience;
I do not understand your ways,
but you know the way for me. . . .

Restore me to liberty,
And enable me so to live now
that I may answer before you and before me.
Lord, whatever this day may bring,
Your name be praised.

DIETRICH BONHOEFFER,
Prayers of the Martyrs

(Dietrich Bonhoeffer was a German Lutheran pastor and theologian. Arrested in 1943 by the Nazis, he was hanged in a concentration camp by the personal order of Heinrich Himmler in 1945.)

Contents

Part Two: Walking the Path of Prayer

Part Three: Continuing on Through Praise

Acknowledgments

U nforgettable thoughts should never be forgotten.
When I looked back over the manuscript for this book, I recognized timeless stories and insights from some of my favorite friends and authors. You, too, will notice that Charles H. Spurgeon through his unforgettable sermons inspired much of the content. If I had been around in his day, I would have sat in the front row of his church every Sunday.

For this reason, I must thank Baker Book House for "letting Spurgeon live" through publishing his *Twelve Sermons on Prayer.* Snatches of thoughts are included from my book, *Secret Strength,* so special thanks goes to Multnomah Press. Also, I'm grateful to Zondervan Publishing House and Steve Estes—the insights shared in *A Step Further* are still having an impact for the Lord Jesus as new and different readers enjoy this book.

Finally, I'm grateful to Jim Galvin and Angela Hunt, along with Bev Singleton, for helping to give shape to my words and, ultimately, to people's prayers.

Part One

Starting Your Journey

One

Preparing Your Heart
To Seek God

> But if . . . you seek the LORD your God, you
> will find him if you look for him with all your
> heart and with all your soul.
>
> DEUTERONOMY 4:29

It's tough being a teenager. It's even tougher when you're seventeen and face life in a wheelchair. I receive a lot of letters from thirteen-, fourteen-, and fifteen-year-olds, and many of them honestly feel they should end it all. They simply can't face the fact that an injury has paralyzed their legs or an accident has taken away their sight.

Even though a couple of decades have passed since I was that age, all those feelings and memories are as fresh as if they happened yesterday. Maybe that's because "life on my feet" stopped when I was seventeen, when I broke my neck in a diving accident.

The toughest part of those early days in the hospital was living up to my reputation as a Christian when people came to visit me. I felt like people expected me to put on a happy face. Try as I might, I just couldn't. My failure made me feel even more guilty about letting down my parents, my pastor, and my Christian friends. Being newly injured, I suddenly realized there was a lot more to all those Bible verses I had learned in Sunday school. Romans 8:28, "all things work together for good" (KJV), had always served me well when I was on my feet. Of course, my toughest problem in those days was sweating out fifty sit-ups in gym class or arguing with my sister after she borrowed my clothes. Hardship meant staying up late to cram for an algebra test.

Would all those Sunday school verses work now that I had to sit in a wheelchair? I wasn't so sure. Being in that hospital, I felt like I got hit with a sudden dose of "growing up," and I didn't like it one bit.

But at night, after everyone else had gone home, I would pray, "God, if I can't die, show me how to live, please!" It was short, to the point, but it was a prayer voiced straight from my heart.

Things didn't change overnight, but with that simple prayer my outlook began to change. I realized that "growing up" was just something I was going to have to learn how to do. I would have to learn how to do the impossible—handle life in a wheelchair.

You might not have the strength to say much more to God than a simple prayer like "show me how to live." But God is not looking for a lot of fancy words. He can take that simple desire of your heart and start you on a spiritual journey of prayer and praise that will be richer than anything you ever dreamed would be possible.

Psalm 34:18 says, "The LORD is close to the brokenhearted and saves those who are crushed in spirit." You may not change overnight with such a simple prayer, but right now you can ask God to show you how to live. Pray it and mean it. And then watch your outlook change. You just might start living the impossible.

Prayer Moves God

It's been said that faith may move mountains, but prayer moves God. Amazing, isn't it, that our prayers, whether grand and glorious or feeble and faint, can move the very heart of God who created the universe? To walk with God we must make it a practice to talk with God, and that's what this book is all about: seeking God on a spiritual journey of prayer and praise.

Prayer moves God, and when God moves in your life, things get exciting! Years ago I never dreamed that God would move in my life the way He has. Even after my accident, when I signed up at the University of Maryland for art and English classes, I never realized how God would use diverse elements in my life

---

"Prayer moves God, and when God moves in your life, things get exciting!"

---

to mold me to His will. But I sensed God was preparing me for something, and He started me out on a spiritual journey of prayer and praise that has not yet ended. You, too, have a journey through life ahead. Why not make it a journey of prayer and praise?

I'm not perfect; I'm still learning about prayer. God is still revealing His plan for me, and He and I are still in this adventure of life together. But I've learned a few lessons I'd like to share with you in the hopes that your prayer life will become richer.

The Importance of Prayer

I am a good visual aid to illustrate how important a healthy prayer life is. My mind has some great ideas for my hands and legs to carry out, but there has been a break in the communication system—my hands and legs just can't carry out what my mind asks them to do. Colossians 2:19 describes men who have "lost connection with the Head, from whom the whole body, supported and held together by its ligaments and sinews, grows as God causes it to grow."

A healthy spiritual body of believers should take their direction from Christ, their Head, just as individual Christians should maintain the communication system with Christ. Without communication with our Head, Jesus Christ, we grow ineffective and our spiritual muscles atrophy.

Prayer is the hub of that communication. Prayer is the pause that empowers. It is the one weapon our enemy, the devil, cannot duplicate or counterfeit. It is not measured by its length but by its depth. Effective prayer doesn't require a Ph.D.—it only requires a willingness to share your thoughts with God.

Holding On to the Belt of Truth

This chapter is about having a heart prepared for prayer. And if there's one truth about prayer, it's this: Hang on to truth. Hang on to it for dear life.

Think about it. Have you ever held on to something as though your life depended on it? I have. When I was four years old, I used to go horseback riding with my family. I'm not talking about sitting on some small pony being led around a little ring. I'm talking about wild and woolly, galloping jaunts up and down hills and through pastures, jumping fences, and splashing through streams. Real horseback riding.

At four, I was too young to have my own horse, and I'm not sure a pony fit for a four year old could have kept up with my father and sisters, anyway. So when we went horseback riding, I sat behind my father on his big horse. With my tiny hands, I'd hang on to his belt for dear life, and off we'd go! I'd bounce up and down on the back of his saddle, sliding this way and that, but as long as I had a strong hold on that belt, I knew I was safe.

That memory came back to me recently when I was reading Ephesians 6, that portion of Scripture where Paul talks about the armor of God. Paul tells us to put on the breastplate of righteousness and the helmet of salvation and take up the sword of the Spirit.

"If there's one truth about prayer, it's this: Hang on to truth. Hang on to it for dear life."

Paul mentions a very important part of the armor in verse 14: "Stand firm then, with the *belt of truth* buckled around your waist" (emphasis added). The belt of truth, especially in prayer, is like a foundation. We put it on before we put on other things, and if there's anything we ought to not lose grip on, it should be the belt of truth. The Bible says we are to approach God "in spirit and in truth" (John 4:24). Another way of putting that: Approach God in prayer with heartfelt honesty.

Now I'm not too much different from when I was a child. When the going gets rough and I feel I'm being led up and down, this way and that, I know I've got that belt. There are truths about God that I can hold on to. God is in control. He leads me in a righteous path. Nothing can touch me that is not in His plan. He's interested in my highest good. He has blessed me with every spiritual blessing. His grace, available and abundant, more than sustains. These are the strands that weave the belt of truth, and as long as I hold on, I'm going to be safe in my spiritual journey.

Job's Story

Job had a firm grip on the belt of truth, and his story has always been an inspiration to me. Some people say the book of Job is about suffering. Others say it's a story of faith or the sovereignty of God or the relationship between God and the devil, but I think the book of Job is about prayer. Consider Job's cry:

> If only I knew where to find him; if only I could go to his dwelling! I would state my case before him and fill my mouth with arguments. I would find out what he would answer me, and consider what he would say. (Job 23:3–5)

You know the story of Job. He was an upright and righteous man, a man blessed of God. He had seven sons and three daughters, and he owned seven thousand sheep, three thousand camels, five hundred oxen, five hundred donkeys, and had a large number of servants. He was, the Bible tells us, "the greatest man among all the people of the East" (Job 1:3).

Job was a godly father to his children, a humble man before his neighbors, and a priest to his large household. But then Satan took aim at Job.

Job was feeling as though he were the target in a cosmic game of darts between God and the devil. His property was either ruined or stolen, and his family killed. He was covered with boils, and he sat in a big pile of ashes, surrounded by critical friends and a nagging wife. He had a lot to talk to God about.

Job's Right Reaction

Job's friends gathered around for seven days of silent sympathy, then they began prying. "Come on, Job," they said. "Surely you've done something terribly wrong and this is God's discipline. 'Fess up, and tell us all about it."

Then Job prayed. But listen to his prayer—he didn't pray, "Oh, that I might be healed of these boils," or "Oh, that I might have my children back," or even, "Oh, that these friends and my wife would get off my back!" Instead, Job's desire was to see the Father's face and to feel His smile. "If only I knew where to find him!" Job prayed, "I would state my case before him . . . and consider what he would say."

This may seem off the subject, but think: What do you get when you squeeze an orange? Orange juice? Maybe, if no one

---

"It is the heaven-born instinct of a child of God to seek shelter beneath the wings of the Almighty. The tendency to complain or to assert that God owes us something is not spiritual."

---

has tampered with the orange or already squeezed it. When you squeeze an orange, what comes out is whatever is inside!

What happens when life "squeezes" a Christian? What is revealed is whatever is inside. A hypocrite, or someone who simply pretends to be a child of God, resents affliction and runs when troubled times come. His cowardice and pretense come out.

A self-centered Christian may complain for a while, but, in time, affliction can bring him to his knees. Then his heart can be drained of the selfishness and resentment, making him better able to approach God as a child would seek his father.

Some Christians treat God as a kind of insurance agent. In hard times, they expect Him to issue a claim check to restore what they've lost. While waiting for Him to change their circumstances for the better, they withhold fellowship from Him. Life's "squeeze" reveals their lack of submission and stubborn attitudes.

It is the heaven-born instinct of a child of God to seek shelter beneath the wings of the Almighty. The tendency to complain or to assert that God owes us something is not spiritual.

The godly instinct of a child of God is to say with Job, "Oh, that I might find Him."

Job longed for God's presence. God had not left him, nor had He stopped protecting His child, but Job felt as though he had lost the smile of God: "Oh, that I knew where to find Him!"

Have you ever responded the way Job did? You have been obedient. You haven't run in the other direction. You haven't been self-centered or demanded an explanation from God before you agree to worship Him. But you long for His smile. You wish to see His face in the stormy clouds. Your heart aches as you cry, "Oh, that I might find Him!"

That was Job's heartache. Even in despair and distress, the desire of Job's heart was to seek God. And, oh, what a prepared heart for prayer he had. Why? Because he did not lose his grip on those things about God he knew to be true. And it was that Almighty God and the truth of His Word that was the desire of Job's heart.

What a way to begin your spiritual journey of prayer and praise: Desire God.

Prayer Point

Prayer is what communication with God is all about. And what does He require as we approach Him in prayer? Truth. Genuineness. Sincerity. Heartfelt honesty. And please know this to be true of God: When we call on Him in truth, He listens! There's only one reaction you could have toward love so great. In fact, why don't you make it your prayer right now?

Oh Lord, if I were to be wholeheartedly honest with You right now, I'd have to admit I've often run in the other direction when trials squeeze me. At times, I've been a first-class hypocrite. But, like Job, I want to find You; I want to feel Your smile. Help me make that my heart's desire, in Jesus' name.

You're on your way. Your heart is prepared for seeking God in prayer.

For Group Discussion

1. What does it mean to seek God with all your heart and with all your soul? How would you explain this to a new believer?

2. How do you usually prepare your heart for prayer? What would you tell someone who wanted to know how to prepare his or her heart for prayer?

3. When is it difficult for you to pray with heartfelt honesty? What would help you be more honest with God?

4. What do you admire about Job's reaction to his time of crisis? What could you do to make your prayer more like his?

5. What are some of the barriers, events, feelings, or circumstances that prevent you from preparing your heart for prayer? What can you do to overcome them?

6. In what way has your journey through life been one of prayer and praise? What would you like to improve about your prayer and praise?

Two

Seeking Shelter In the Storm

> He who dwells in the shelter of the Most High
> will rest in the shadow of the Almighty. I will
> say of the LORD, "He is my refuge and my for-
> tress, my God, in whom I trust."
>
> PSALM 91:1–2

As you know, I loved horseback riding when I was on my feet, especially when I was little. When I finally was big enough to ride my own pony, I just *had* to keep up with my older sisters on their big horses. My problem was that I was only riding a pony half the size of their mounts, so I had to gallop twice as fast to keep up with everybody else.

I didn't mind doing that—I took it as a challenge, until we came to the edge of a river. My sisters always liked to splash ahead, crossing the river at the deepest part. On their big horses, it was fun. But they never seemed to notice that my pony and I were a lot smaller and that we sunk quite a bit deeper into the swirling waters. I was scared, but I wasn't about to let them know.

I'll never forget one river crossing. It was the Gorsuch Switch Crossing at the Patapsco River. Rain earlier in the week had swollen the river to the brim of its bank. As our horses waded out toward midstream, I stared at the rushing waters that swirled around the shaking legs of my pony. Mesmerized by the circling waters, I felt dizzy. I was frightened and began to lose my balance in the saddle.

My sister—Jay—called back to me. "Look up, Joni—keep looking up!" Sure enough, as soon as I took my eyes off the water and focused on my sister, I regained my balance and finished the river crossing.

That river crossing came to mind recently when I was reading about Peter in Matthew 14. It seems Peter had the same problem when he was walking on the water toward the Lord Jesus. He looked down at the raging waves, got dizzy, and lost his balance. Because he took his eyes off the Lord, he began to sink.

We are so much like Peter! Instead of keeping our eyes on the Word of God, we often let our circumstances transfix us, absorbing us to the point where we lose our spiritual equilibrium. We become dizzy with fear and anxiety. Before we know it, we've lost our balance.

I'm sure there have been times when you've lost your balance in prayer. You try hard to bundle your anxieties and lay them at the feet of Jesus, but you find yourself distracted, absorbed even, by the very concerns you want to pray about.

Am I describing you? Feeling a little panic, are you? Don't know what to do when all your children get sick? Can't seem to adjust to life without wheels while your car is getting a new transmission? Are the books just not balancing this month? Maybe your teenager brought some new "friends" home yesterday, and you're worried about what kind of friends they really are.

It's easy to panic, isn't it? Admittedly, it's hard to look up—especially when you feel like you're sinking.

But I made it across the river, and Peter made it back to his boat. Thousands before you have made it through, keeping their eyes on the Lord Jesus. How about you? If you can't find a way out, try looking up. Look up in prayer! And what do you see when you look up? Jesus. Fix your eyes on Jesus.

You may have to keep refocusing your attention, pulling your eyes off the swirling circumstances that overwhelm you. As you steady your gaze upon the Lord, you will regain your balance.

"We are so much like Peter! Instead of keeping our eyes on the Word of God, we often let our circumstances transfix us, absorbing us to the point where we lose our spiritual equilibrium."

When We Feel Small and Insignificant

I can just hear you saying, "Joni, it sounds good, but you don't know my circumstances. God may be big, but my problems are huge. I try to pray, but I feel so small."

I felt that way a couple of years ago when Ken and I fit a few days of mountain camping into our busy schedule. We pitched our tent under some tall, straight sequoias near a mountain creek still flowing swiftly with melted snow from the High Sierras. It was breathtaking. Crisp, cold mornings made the aroma of fresh mountain trout sizzling over the breakfast campfire smell even better.

Ken and I don't do anything fancy on our camping trips. For me, it's a flannel shirt, dusty jeans, no makeup, and a bandanna over dirty hair. I love it!

One morning we rented a boat on a lake brimming with trout. The glacial spires of craggy rock which framed our lake pulled the breath from our lungs. Drifting around in our little rowboat, surrounded by soaring mountain peaks, wide blue water, and blustery winds, I felt small.

As we floated in the morning stillness, I thought of Job. He had argued his case before God, and it was time for God to answer. Job must have felt very small on the day when Almighty God crossed mountains and lakes to come down to question him.

God asked him, "Where were you when I laid the earth's foundation? . . . Who marked off its dimensions? . . . Who laid its cornerstone—while the morning stars sang together and all the angels shouted for joy?" (Job 38:4–7).

I stared at the white-capped mountains above me and thought of how God went on to query Job about whose power formed ice and snow. Then God asked, "Does the eagle soar at your command and build his nest on high?" (Job 39:27). Those words from the book of Job came to mind when an eagle caught my eye as he left his nest in one of the rocky crags to swoop over our lake in search of a fish.

Yes, the mountains, the snow, the hawks and eagles, the clouds and wind all have a way of making us feel so small, almost insignificant—just as Job must have felt.

But there's another side of the story to consider. As marvelous as mountains, proud eagles, ancient glaciers, and the mighty panorama of wind and clouds are, I am not so small that God, the great Creator, did not strip Himself of all His divine trappings and humble Himself to save me.

As it says in Philippians 2:7, Jesus "made himself nothing, taking the very nature of a servant, being made in human likeness" for me. Jesus became "small" so that I might be "great" in Him.

Sure, you've been overshadowed by larger-than-life realities. Yes, there have been times when you've cringed like Job, thinking that you're so small, you're simply—nothing. Little wonder you've found it hard to pray. But please don't give up. Don't be overwhelmed. Recognize that the same God who towers above and around you also humbled Himself and became a man. He who spoke the High Sierras into being whispers to you . . . in prayer. He formed the mighty mountains, had a hand in forming your overwhelming circumstances, and is ready to talk to you about it in prayer.

Feel small and insignificant if you must, but know this: You are not small in His eyes.

God Is an Ever-Present Refuge

To tell you the truth, there are times when I'm relieved, glad even, that I feel small next to God. After all, when you feel small, you want to run to something, someone who is big. It's safe next to a rock, a fortress, a stronghold. You can feel safe in prayer because God is all these strong places to you.

I know something about fortresses. I have happy childhood memories of my sister Kathy and me constructing a tree house on the farm. Our little fortress was some distance from the farmhouse, so it was private and far away from adults. We worked hard lugging wood, confiscating nails, and borrowing hammers to construct a very sturdy tree house.

To my childlike way of thinking, that tree house was a fortress. Not just a shelter or a place to hide, but a safe house that would protect us from the rain beating on the tin roof and the wind shaking the branches of the tree. We were safe. We felt secure.

Wouldn't it be nice if that oh-so-safe feeling could be found as easily today? In our adult world, there aren't many "tree houses" where we can feel secure. But there is one such place, and it's more than a fragile refuge of our own making.

Scripture tells us:

The LORD is my rock, my fortress and my deliverer; my God is my rock, in whom I take refuge. He is my shield and the horn of my salvation, my stronghold. I call to the LORD, who is worthy of praise, and I am saved from my enemies. (Psalm 18:2–3)

So we say with confidence, " The Lord is my helper; I will not be afraid. What can man do to me?" (Hebrews 13:6)

There's a lot more safety and security in the Lord than in safe-houses of our own making and design. That little tree house gave new meaning to the words *refuge* or *high tower.* Now that I'm an adult, I put childish activities behind me and go—I hope you do, too—to a place, a Person, who is the Everlasting Rock, the High Fortress, the Mighty Fortress, a Tower of Refuge, a Shield and Savior.

When the storms of life crowd in, climb up into His love in prayer.

The Shadow of a Mighty Rock

When I pray, I like to picture myself, small and insignificant, huddling in the comforting shadow of Almighty God as though He were an actual fortress, a high tower directly above me. It's easier to pray when I feel that protected, that sheltered.

Shadows do that. There's something cool and resting when you sit in a shadow—especially on a hot, sweltering day.

You know what I'm talking about. It's like a hot day at the beach. A big umbrella can be the most important piece of paraphernalia you pack. Or when you're sitting on a sticky, hot grandstand seat, a baseball game program provides great shade for your forehead. Or when the distance between your car and the shopping mall seems like an asphalt desert, a wide-brimmed hat is exactly what you need.

Nothing cools and refreshes like a sliver of shade when we're feeling the heat. In the same way, there's nothing like the refreshing comfort of the shadow of God's presence which does not shift or change.

I like the way the psalmist describes the experience:

O God, you are my God, earnestly I seek you; my soul thirsts for you, my body longs for you, in a dry and weary land where there is no water. . . . Because you are my help, I sing in the shadow of your wings. (Psalm 63:1,7)

"When I pray, I like to picture myself,
small and insignificant, huddling in the
comforting shadow of Almighty God as
though He were an actual fortress, a
high tower directly above me."

Prayer Point

Right now, recall the last time you found the shelter of shade on a hot day. Remember how rested you felt from the energy-sapping sun? List in your mind those feelings: Unburdened. Relieved. Consoled. Comforted.

Now, that's the way you can feel in the sheltering shade of the Most High God. Rested. Unburdened. Secure. You can breathe in God's shadow.

Take a moment to come before God in prayer and picture yourself in His shadow. Imagine yourself finding a safe place in the cleft of the Rock. Now, fix your eyes on Jesus and bring to Him those problems, those overwhelming circumstances that distract you. Wrap words around those worries of yours and list them one by one as you lay them in His shadow.

Then enjoy that unburdened feeling in His shade. Close your prayer with the psalmist, *"He is my refuge and my fortress, my God, in whom I trust"* (Psalm 91:2).

For Group Discussion

1. As a child, what gave you a sense of security (blanket, stuffed animal, etc.)? What gives you security now?

2. What possible future crises could undermine your security and cause you to panic?

3. How can prayer help you feel safe and secure?

4. In what situations do you often feel small and insignificant? How does prayer make you feel small and important at the same time?

5. When do you need a refuge, a place that protects you and makes you feel safe?

6. How is God your refuge? How does prayer place you in God's safe house?

Three

Seeking God
With Carefulness

Our prayers must mean something to us if they
are to mean anything to God.

MALTBIE D. BABCOCK

Hebrews 13:9 says, "It is good for our hearts to be strength-
ened by grace." In other words, we're strong when we
have God's grace. God's grace is good for our hearts.

But what is grace? Some theologians have said that grace is
GOD'S RICHES AT CHRIST'S EXPENSE. Some commentaries say
that grace is God's unmerited favor. Others have described
grace as the agent through which God gives us the desire and
power to do His will. These are man's best attempts to define
what is nearly impossible for us to understand—God's grace.

But how do we get grace? How does God go about dispens-
ing it? Well, it's nice to know that grace is a free gift. But there
are a few things to remember as we take hold of His gift. First,
God wants us to be humble as we come to Him for grace. After
all, Scripture tells us that "God opposes the proud but gives
grace to the humble" (James 4:6).

That's important to keep in mind because there are lots of
Christians, myself included, who thoughtlessly meander up to
God as though He were a doting old grandfather in the sky,

giving out grace as He would pass out chocolate chip cookies. You know, the ask-and-it's-ours attitude. What a bunch of spoiled brats we must seem when we ask with a "gimme" mind-set!

Approaching an Awesome God

How, then, should we approach God in prayer?

A popular song reminds us that "our God is an awesome God." In today's vernacular, *awesome* means something akin to "super cool," but our God is "awesome" in the sense that He has the power to inspire dread and profound and humbly fearful reverence. We should be properly terrified before the Lord our holy God; we should feel wonder and reverent fear.

Job knew the power of his awesome God. As Job desired the presence of his God, he carefully planned how he would order his cause and state his case before the Lord: "Oh that I knew where I might find him! . . . I would order my cause before him, and fill my mouth with arguments" (Job 23:3–4, KJV). He did not intend to approach God carelessly or with accusations. He understood the significance of prayer and the power of Him who sat on the throne.

There's a widespread notion today that prayer is easy. Too many of us pray carelessly. We have "habitual" prayers that we murmur before bed or at meals, simple little phrases like "God bless us all and thanks for the food and the good day and forgive us because we've sinned again." We shuffle up to the throne of God, yawning and muttering the first thing that comes to mind. We casually utter our praises, our petitions, our thanksgivings, our supplications—hardly stopping to think before we open our mouths.

There's danger in doing that, I'm afraid, because there is power in what we say before the throne of God's grace. We must approach with a kind of holy carefulness. I learned that lesson the hard way.

> "We should be properly terrified before
> the Lord our holy God; we should feel
> wonder and reverent fear."

God Answered My Prayer

I accepted Christ when I was a fourteen-year-old kid on a Young Life weekend retreat. But I immediately pushed God to a corner of my mind and placed Him in a box labeled, "Break in case of emergency." I went to God as if He were a spiritual vending machine into which I fed dime-like prayers and pulled levers. I didn't know if my requests were spiritual or scriptural. I just casually sauntered up to the throne of God's grace and punched in my requests.

That attitude got me into trouble. I began to experience discouragement and despondency in my walk with the Lord Jesus. There was no victory over sin for me. I was exasperated, yet my prayers only became more and more self-centered: "Lord, help me lose fifteen pounds now that I'm Your child," or "Lord, help me get through my homework tonight and help it not to be so boring," or "Lord, I sure do like that guy who's captain of the football team. Could You get me a date with him?"

One Friday evening when I didn't have a date, I was particularly frustrated. I had a new pimple on my chin. I felt overweight and ugly. I threw myself on my bed and cried. I clasped my Bible to my chest and said, "Oh, God, do something in my life, just do something. I don't care what happens, but I don't like being miserable!"

I prayed that prayer without knowing how God would answer it. I thought He would introduce me to a Bible camp counselor that summer who would help me straighten my life out. Maybe I would meet some strong Christian guy who would help me get deeper into God's Word. Or then again, there was a chance I would find a really good fellowship group on my college campus that fall. Perhaps God would make me into a missionary. Maybe I would end up at a Bible college.

To my way of thinking, all these possibilities were reasonable answers to my request to get closer to God. After all, some of my Christian friends had prayed for a closer walk with Jesus, and the Lord had done such things in their lives. So I began looking for the different direction my life would take that last year in high school.

My life *did* take a different direction, but there was no way I could have prepared myself for the surprise—no, the downright shock—that awaited me.

You see, God took my prayer seriously. About a month later, I dived recklessly into shallow water. When I hit bottom and broke my neck, eerily my life flashed before my eyes, and I knew God was answering that prayer. I was only seventeen years old, but I knew that this accident was, in a strange way, the answer to my prayer.

I confess, though, that weeks later as I lay on a Stryker frame in the hospital, facing a life of sitting in a wheelchair without the use of my hands or legs, I fumed, "Great God, this is Your idea of an answer to prayer? Believe me, I will never trust You with another prayer again!"

Petition with Careful Respect

Although I wouldn't have called it a legitimate answer to prayer back then, I now see that it was. I can't deny it—God has drawn me closer to Him through my injury. My wheelchair, whether I like it or not, forces me to seek out His Word. It didn't happen through a Bible college or a summer camp. It happened through months of struggling on a hospital Stryker frame. Prayer, as you can see, is serious business. When we approach the throne of God's grace, we have to be careful and approach with a kind of holy carefulness . . . a conscientious piety. If you don't think you need to foster that kind of sharpened attitude toward prayer, let me challenge you with the following example.

Suppose a man receives a traffic ticket he thinks he didn't deserve. He follows instructions on how to appeal the ticket and leaves work in the middle of the day for his scheduled court

---

"God has drawn me closer to Him through my injury. My wheelchair, whether I like it or not, forces me to seek out His Word."

---

appearance. Trouble is, he leaves wearing his work clothes—a casual short-sleeved shirt and jeans. He considers the entire affair a waste of time and a capital annoyance.

His attitude is apparent in court. Before the proceedings even begin, he meanders up to the judge's bench, leans on his elbow, cracks his gum, and says to the judge, "Look, you're a nice guy and you gotta understand this whole thing stinks."

The judge looks at the traffic ticket, eyes the well-groomed policeman off to the side, and then stares down at the petitioner. "The citation stands," the judge rules curtly.

The petitioner makes the mistake of rolling his eyes. "Young man, would you like to be held in contempt of court?" the judge demands.

The petitioner gets the message and announces, in a subdued voice, that he would still like to appeal the traffic citation.

In his next court appearance, the man with the traffic ticket wears his best suit. He makes a genuine effort to appear concerned and responsible, he organizes his facts and articulates his side of the story in a polite and thoughtful manner. The traffic ticket is dismissed with no problem. The judge saw his side of the story and justice prevailed.

If you were called into court as a witness or even a defendant, would you stop and think before speaking? Of course. After all, no petitioner enters court thinking that he can state his case on the spur of the moment.

A wise petitioner will enter the chamber with his case well prepared and his ideas well thought out. He wouldn't dare talk off the top of his head. He would never prop his feet up on the railing, lean back in his chair, put his hands behind his head, yawn, or utter the first thing that comes to mind. No, he'd prepare his case or hire a professional lawyer to do it for him.

So why do we often pray so carelessly, even sloppily? Take a look at the Old Testament. The priests who approached God had an attitude of holy carefulness. When they offered sacrifices for the people, they were not to rush into God's presence. The priests would kill the bull, wash their feet, put on garments and special vestments, approach the altar with the bull properly portioned, sprinkle the blood in a certain place, and light the fire a prescribed way with one—and only one—certain kind of match.

Why were the sacrifices so detailed? The underlying truth was simple: Think before you pray.

Prayers Are Offerings, Too

Our prayers are spiritual sacrifices, too. Often we think of God as a Supreme Being who happily sits by a celestial telephone, only too thrilled when we call and list our demands. I've heard preachers who say, "All you have to do is name it and claim it. You can demand from God what is rightfully yours."

Yes, God may answer demands much as He answered the demands of the children of Israel when they tempted Him in the wilderness. He gave them their requests; but remember that He also sent leanness into their souls.

Where do we get this idea that God is overjoyed to comply with our demands? True, God is our best friend, but we dare not take His friendship for granted. Yes, God is happy and willing to hear each of our requests. But the Bible tells us that we are to "worship God acceptably with reverence and awe, for our 'God is a consuming fire' " (Hebrews 12:28–29).

"When we acknowledge God as God, we do not 'claim.' We must not demand. It is better to thoughtfully 'let your requests be made known unto God' (Philippians 4:6, KJV), . . . [to] have an attitude of submission, of humility, of deference to the King of kings and Lord of lords."

When we acknowledge God as God, we do not "claim." We must not demand. It is better to thoughtfully "let your requests be made known unto God" (Philippians 4:6, KJV). Then we have an attitude of submission, of humility, of deference to the King of kings and Lord of lords.

Yes, there are lots of folks who name it and claim it and demand it and receive it. But frankly, when I look down at this wheelchair, it's a not-so-subtle reminder that God will take very seriously the words we utter before His throne of grace. So it's the wise people who preface prayer with a Thy-will-be-done attitude as they submissively let their requests be made known to God.

Mercy and Grace at the Throne

Hebrews 4:16 gives us good advice: "Let us then approach the throne of grace with confidence, so that we may receive mercy and find grace to help us in our time of need." You ought to underline that verse in your Bible if you haven't done so already. It describes the kind of attitude we need to have when we approach God's throne in prayer. Notice the wording: First we receive mercy, then we find grace. That's a great clue as to what our attitude in prayer ought to be.

We may go to God, looking for grace to see us through our problems, but first we must approach our awesome God to receive mercy. Before we obtain answers to our petitions, wants, desires, or requests, we need to humble ourselves so that we may find His favor. That's the attitude we need.

Prayer Point

Charles Spurgeon said, "He who prays without fervency does not pray at all. We cannot commune with God, who is a consuming fire, if there is no fire in our prayers."

What one of us wouldn't want fire in our prayers? You can have it, you know, when you approach God in careful holiness, first to obtain mercy and then to find grace to help you as you pray.

Right now, imagine yourself in the great throne room of God. Picture the surroundings—the great walls, the tapestries, the throne, the thousands of angels worshiping. Set yourself in the scene as you approach your Almighty God with your praise and petition. Kneel before Him in your heart. Quiet your thoughts. Center your thinking. Focus your words, and then in submission and humility, let your requests be made known to Him.

For Group Discussion

1. How do Christians sometimes act like spoiled brats when they pray?

2. What are some examples of careless habitual prayers? In what other ways are we too casual in our relationship with God?

3. What does it mean to be properly terrified before the Lord? Why is prayer serious business?

4. How have your prayers changed as you've grown in your faith?

5. How can you approach God with confidence as well as reverence?

6. What will help you remember to pray with reverence?

Four

Seeking God from Dust
And Ashes

> The more we pray, the more we shall want to
> pray. The more we pray, the more we can pray.
> The more we pray, the more we shall pray. He
> who prays little will pray less, but he who prays
> much will pray more. And he who prays more,
> will desire to pray more abundantly.
>
> CHARLES HADDON SPURGEON

I sometimes have a problem when I pray. Maybe I've been disobedient or lax in reading God's Word. Sometimes I try to pray and I'm still fuming over a spat with Ken. There are times when I'm just feeling out of sorts, dull or dry.

Prayer, I realize, is a part of the answer, so I begin to talk with God. But then an old habit crops up. Maybe it's happened to you, too. My mind starts playing games, telling me things like, *Come on, now, God wants to see a little repentance before He helps you out of this mess. Let's get a bit more emotionally involved in this prayer, otherwise God won't think you're serious. . . . God is probably so sick and tired of your piddling around with your Christian walk that He's hidden Himself from you, anyway. And that sin of yours? He's not going to forgive you with a snap of the finger. It just doesn't work that way!*

31

Sound familiar? Well, if you brood over those notions long enough, you'll throw in the towel and quit praying, more discouraged than you were before you began.

When needling accusations hit me, I do my best to remember two verses from Isaiah. The first one is: "Yet the LORD longs to be gracious to you; he rises to show you compassion. For the LORD is a God of justice. Blessed are all who wait for him!" (Isaiah 30:18).

That verse is a favorite when I feel discouraged in prayer. It reminds me that God is just and, at the same time, longs to show graciousness and compassion. That's wonderfully comforting.

Then there's Isaiah 45:19: "I have not spoken in secret, from somewhere in a land of darkness; I have not said to Jacob's descendants, 'Seek me in vain.' I, the LORD, speak the truth; I declare what is right."

When we truly desire mercy, God is ready to be found. There are no cat-and-mouse games to be played in prayer. If we seek Him, He promises our efforts won't be in vain. If we desire grace, He longs to give it to us. If we want comfort, He rises to show compassion.

My First Steps Toward Seeking God

People often ask me, "Joni, what most helped you get your spiritual act together when you were in the hospital? What were the steps? What Bible verses were you told? What pushed you and got you started on your spiritual journey?"

That's tough to answer. I don't like to give trite, prepackaged responses like "Read this passage, then these two psalms, and you'll understand."

Our spiritual journey is a mystery. But there is one experience that, indeed, was significant.

You see, for the longest time I tried to twist God's arm so He'd reveal *why* I had my accident. I was banging on the doors of heaven, demanding an answer to prayer, a reason for my horrible plight. I was insistent, almost belligerent, with God. All the haggling didn't quiet my anxieties or soothe my fears in the middle of the night when I was alone. I was scared and very distraught.

"When we truly desire mercy, God is ready to be found. There are no cat-and-mouse games to be played in prayer."

During those lonely midnight hours I didn't feel so cocky and arrogant in front of God. At those times I pictured Jesus visiting me. I'd imagine Him wearing a rough burlap cloak and a rope belt tied tightly around His waist. My mind's eye saw Him walking softly past the beds of my sleeping roommates, leaving dusty prints from His sandals on the linoleum floor. I'd comfort myself with the image of Him standing at my bedside, lowering the guard rail, and then sitting on the edge of my mattress.

The sharp pain of loneliness was eased as I pictured Jesus leaning over, rubbing my cheek with the backside of His hand, fingering away strands of hair from my face. He'd question me, His eyes fixed on mine: "Joni, if I loved you enough to die for you, don't you think I knew what I was doing when I answered your prayer for a closer walk with Me?"

His reasoning made sense. If Jesus would die for me, then He could be trusted with everything else He would do with my life. That thought alone humbled me before God. The same God who ladled out seas, carved out rivers, pushed up mountain ranges, and dreamed up time and space cared enough to console me.

First Peter 5:6 instructs, "Humble yourselves, therefore, under God's mighty hand, that he may lift you up in due time." Even as I lay there paralyzed, it occurred to me that I had more than enough reason to be grateful. Christ died for me out of love . . . love I didn't deserve.

What happened after that? God began to answer my prayer for a closer walk with Him. Remember my telling you about that prayer I had so carelessly tossed up: "Oh, God, I want to get close to You"? Only after I humbled myself before the Lord did He begin to lift me up. Slowly and steadily, God began to lift me up out of my anxiety and fear. It didn't happen overnight, but that beginning lift was the push I needed.

Dust and Ashes

"Now that I have been so bold as to speak to the Lord, though I am nothing but dust and ashes" (Genesis 18:27)—that was Abraham's attitude when he prayed. I'm struck with his attitude of humility. And the lower Abraham humbled himself, the "higher" he must have felt. I can imagine that when Abraham spoke to God, he felt as though he were carried up on eagle's wings to the heights of heaven. It must have awed him to be allowed, of all things, access to God Almighty. I'm sure even as he spoke to the Lord, he felt as though he were grasping heaven in his arms. He had spoken to the Lord of the universe. That thought alone was enough to lay him lower, reminding him he was mere "dust and ashes."

Dust and ashes. There have been times when I haven't always tasted dust and ashes in prayer, when I haven't glimpsed heaven. Often, my prayers have been more along the line of a neat and orderly arrangement of words around an acronym of Adoration, Confession, Thanksgiving, and Supplication, followed by an Amen. I've been guilty of being far too careful to follow a proper progression of praise and petition, my words all lined up like ducks in a tidy row.

When I look at Abraham's cry to God—a cry that had nothing to do with a mere arrangement of appropriate words—it's clear that spiritually ordered prayers consist of something more than clustering our requests in a tidy, prescribed fashion. Spiritual prayers have to do with praying to a real person, someone

---

"Humbling ourselves in dust and ashes means gaining a sense of our meagerness and God's greatness, our sin and His purity, our humanity and His divinity."

---

who is truly present with us even though we cannot see Him. Spiritual praying is conversing with the unseen Creator of the universe as though He were standing visibly and terribly in front of us. That, if anything, will make us feel like Abraham—amazed that we could be bold enough to speak to God.

Certainly there will be times when we pray "on the run," speaking to God sincerely, yet conversationally. We may offer "shotgun prayers"—quick, earnest petitions or intercessions shared hurriedly, yet from the heart. But when it concerns our regular, daily, committed time of prayer, we will want to take time to examine our heart attitude thoroughly, remembering who we are—and who God is.

Humbling ourselves in dust and ashes means gaining a sense of our meagerness and God's greatness, our sin and His purity, our humanity and His divinity. Cultivating such an attitude will help us better appreciate God's very real presence with us in prayer. Whether we then "see" Jesus sitting on the side of our bed or grasp heaven as did Abraham, our prayers will seem real. They won't be a mechanical arrangement but will be divinely ordered. We will know the assurance of talking to Someone who is really there.

How long has it been since you've felt dust and ashes in prayer? If talking to God doesn't strike you as being one of the most profound, extraordinary privileges imaginable, then perhaps Genesis 18 would be a good place to refresh your prayer life. Only when we feel the dust and ashes can we enter the treasure house of God and embrace heaven.

> In praying, we are often occupied with ourselves, with our own needs, and our own efforts in the presentation of them. In waiting upon God, the first thought is of *the God upon whom we wait*. God longs to reveal Himself, to fill us with Himself. Before you pray, bow quietly before God, to remember and realize who He is, how near He is, how certainly He can and will help. Be still before Him, and allow His Holy Spirit to waken and stir up in your soul the childlike disposition of absolute dependence and confident expectation. Wait on God till you know you have met Him; prayer will then become so different. (Andrew Murray)

When you pray, do you take at least a moment to think about God before you start speaking to Him? Take time this week to concentrate on God *before* you open your mouth to pray. Realize you are addressing a living and holy Being who is actually listening. And then, confess. Take several moments to think back on your day's misdoings, the small and not-so-small transgressions. Then realize that God, if He were so inclined, could destroy you with His white-hot wrath; yet He has chosen to be kind and merciful. His amazing grace is enough to humble us.

He is our loving heavenly Father, full of grace, and we are . . . dust and ashes.

Prayer Point

The pathway to dust and ashes is through humility. It's not easy to lay ourselves low before God, but we begin with praise and confession. Have a hard time couching your regret over sin in honest words? Sometimes, it helps to borrow the words of others when humbling ourselves before the Lord.

Pause right now and consider your great and holy God. Then list in your mind five things you've done today that, you believe, offended or grieved Him. Get down in the dust and ashes and share from your heart this confession from the Book of Common Prayer:

Almighty and most merciful Father; We have erred and strayed from thy ways, like lost sheep. We have followed too much the devices and desires of our own hearts. We have offended against thy holy laws. We have left undone those things which we ought to have done; And we have done those things which we ought not to have done; And there is no health in us. But thou, O Lord, have mercy upon us, miserable offenders. Spare thou those, O God, who confess their faults. Restore thou those who are penitent; According to thy promises declared unto mankind in Christ Jesus our Lord. And grant, O most merciful Father, for His sake; That we may hereafter live a godly, righteous, and sober life, To the glory of thy holy Name. Amen.

For Group Discussion

1. What guilty feelings sometimes stop you from praying?

2. When have you been afraid to pray? What were you afraid of?

3. What have you done to overcome barriers to prayer?

4. What does it mean for you to humble yourself when you pray? How does a humble attitude help you when you pray?

5. What attributes of God help you maintain a humble attitude in prayer?

6. How would you pray differently if you were truly humble before God?

Five

Seeking God
With Specific Requests

> If you are sure it is a right thing for which you
> are asking, plead now, plead at noon, plead at
> night, plead on. With cries and tears spread
> out your case. Order your arguments. Back up
> your pleas with reasons. Urge the precious
> blood of Jesus.
>
> CHARLES HADDON SPURGEON

So what can we pray for? Praying from dust and ashes,
with a holy carefulness, what are we to ask for?
After we have quieted our hearts, centered our thinking, taken
time to focus our vision and perhaps even to imagine what it is
like to approach the throne of God's grace, we need to be specific in our prayers.

About ten years ago, I was sitting in church one Sunday
morning. Our pastor, John MacArthur, was off somewhere at a
pastors' conference, and we had a guest speaker. Frankly, this
man's sermon wasn't holding my interest. I hate to admit it, but
I was plain bored.

I suppose I could have let my thoughts wander, but I
thought to myself, *Come on, this is the Lord's Day. It's a Sunday morning worship service. I want to do something that hon-*

ors God. And if I can't get grabbed by this sermon, I'm just going to bring every one of my thoughts under obedience to the Lord Jesus Christ.

So I decided to pray. But I needed a focus, so my eyes fell on the back of a person's head, a man about five or six pews in front of me. I didn't see his face. I didn't know his name. I didn't even know if he knew Christ, but I just decided I would spend the next thirty minutes or so in concentrated prayer for this man, whoever he was. And so I began praying:

O Father in heaven, thank You that You have loved this individual, whoever he is. And God, if he knows You, would You deepen his love for Your Word? And Father, if he doesn't know You, would You have that pastor up there say something of significance about the gospel so he might be brought into Your kingdom? Lord, strengthen this man, whoever he is.

Father, if he's not married and he is dating somebody, don't let him get away with any sexual immorality. Keep him, hold him to his morals. Lord, if he is married, don't let him cheat on his wedding vows. Keep him honorable, would You, God? Don't let those girls in his office, whoever they are, flirt with him. And don't let him be pulled away by temptation.

I stared at the man's head, his hair black and shining, and a wave of peace washed over me as I sensed victory in prayer. I kept praying:

Strengthen this man, would You, God? Refine his faith, keep him from lies, clean up his bad habits, would You? Assist him in prayer and sustain him in health. Guard his mind, God. Lord, would You deepen his friendships, help him to obey, increase his love for You? Lord, if he is having problems with his mom or dad, resolve those conflicts at home, would You? God, help him to get along with his boss or his supervisor at work so he'll be a more honorable witness and testimony to You. Lord, answer his questions, would You, if he has doubts about his faith.

I prayed on and on. After thirty minutes, I can't tell you how excited I was! I was thrilled that I had prayed for this person I

"After we have quieted our hearts, centered our thinking, taken time to focus our vision and perhaps even to imagine what it is like to approach the throne of God's grace, we need to be specific in our prayers."

---

didn't even know. I was worshiping God in this very practical way of being specific.

When the service was over, I thought about making my way down to that man and mentioning my prayer. But no. He'd think I was nuts! Or making advances or something. And I didn't want the morning's victory to be tarnished. I decided to keep my prayer a secret between God and me.

The Answer to Prayer

God surprised me with the rest of the story. I met this man about one month after I had prayed for him in church. Introduced by a mutual friend, I noticed a good-looking Oriental guy with broad shoulders and striking black hair. The hair looked familiar, so I said, "Would you turn around a minute and let me see the back of your head?"

I couldn't believe it! I said, "I can't believe this, but I prayed for you for about half an hour in church about a month ago." He really thought I was a little crazy for doing that, but it sparked his interest—he thought I was unusual. We became friends, and he asked me out on a date. To make a long story short, about eighteen months later we married, and now I am pleased to be the wife of my wonderful husband, Ken Tada.

More Than We Ask or Think

When we are specific in prayer, God "is able to do immeasurably more than all we ask or imagine, according to his power that is at work within us" (Ephesians 3:20). Isn't that marvelous? God wants to do so much more than we could ever ask. When we buckle down and get specific, our sovereign God will do far more than we could ever imagine.

A few years ago I was invited by the Billy Graham Evangelistic Association to lead two workshops during "Amsterdam '86," a large international congress on Third World evangelism. There were evangelists from over 160 countries, including Malawi, Bangladesh, India, the Solomon Islands, Western Samoa, and the Philippines. It was incredible!

Our workshops on sharing Christ with those who are disabled were wonderfully well attended. Between sessions, I was almost hit broadside by an excited evangelist with dark olive skin and a bushy beard. In a thick Middle Eastern accent, he said, "Oh, I must tell you that I am from Iran, and I must tell you that my friends and I translated your books into the Persian language and have been sharing them faithfully with handicapped people in Tehran."

It was all I could do not to cry right in front of the man. When I wrote *Joni* and *A Step Further*, I thought maybe a few disabled people like me, in wheelchairs, could benefit from the message. I figured my relatives might buy a copy. But when that evangelist from Iran told me about a Persian version of my book, it really made me think. I wish I had been a lot more specific in my prayers about the ministry of those books when they were first published. Yet God was doing far more than I could ever ask or even imagine, turning my small, specific request into a grand answer!

"I Will Not Let You Go . . . "

Perhaps you remember the story of Jacob wrestling with God. You'll find it in Genesis 32:24–28. Jacob wrestled with God through the night until daybreak, and God touched Jacob's hip so that his hip was wrenched out of its socket. The man said, "Let me go, for it is daybreak."

"When we are sure what we are asking is for God's glory, not for selfish gain or impure motives, then we can say with Jacob, 'I will not let Thee go except Thou bless me.' "

But Jacob replied, "I will not let you go unless you bless me." Because Jacob persevered, God changed Jacob's name to Israel, because he had "struggled with God and with men and . . . overcome."

Have you struggled with something until you were sure it was God's will? Have you persevered in prayer because you know it is right? Charles Spurgeon said:

It is delightful to hear a man wrestle with God and say, "I will not let Thee go except Thou bless me," but that must be said softly, and not in a hectoring spirit, as though we could command and exact blessings from the Lord of all. Remember, it is still a man wrestling, even though permitted to wrestle with the eternal *I AM*. Jacob halted on his thigh after that night's holy conflict, to let him see that God is terrible, and that his prevailing power did not lie in himself. We are taught to say, "Our Father," but still it is, "Our Father *who art in heaven*." Familiarity there may be, but holy familiarity; boldness, but the boldness which springs from grace and is the work of the Spirit; not the boldness of the rebel who carries a brazen front in the presence of his offended king, but the boldness of the child who fears because he loves, and loves because he fears. (Charles Haddon Spurgeon, *Lectures to My Students*)

I like Martin Luther's prayer: "Lord, I will have my will of Thee at this time, because I know it is Thy will." Have you ever been able to pray that way? When we are sure what we are asking is for God's glory, not for selfish gain or impure motives, then we can say with Jacob, "I will not let Thee go except Thou bless me." It's a risky prayer, isn't it? Some people have broken their necks finding God. Other people like Jacob have had their hips thrown out of socket. But ah, the blessings that come!

Prayer Point

Are there specific questions you want to ask God? Specific areas you need God's help in? Take time now to list them. Then talk to God about them one by one. "Wrestle" with Him over them if you have to. Ask Him to show you His will in each point. Be open to the changes God may bring in your life.

For Group Discussion

1. As you were reading my story about praying for the man in church, how did you think it would end? When have you prayed for strangers?

2. What specific answers to prayer are impressed on your memory? What specific answers to prayer have you received recently?

3. What general prayers that you usually pray could you make more specific? When might prayers be *too* specific?

4. What does it mean to "wrestle with God" in prayer? What benefits come from persisting in prayer?

5. When have you wrestled with God in prayer? How did God change you in the process? How did God answer your prayer?

Six

Seeking to Be Disciplined in Prayer

> I believe that when we cannot pray, it is time that we prayed more than ever. And if you answer, "But how can that be?" I would say, pray to pray. Pray for prayer. Pray for the spirit of supplication. Do not be content to say, "I would pray if I could." No, but if you cannot pray, pray till you can.
>
> CHARLES HADDON SPURGEON

Praying wisely involves the three elements we have discussed in chapters 3, 4, and 5: showing complete submission to the Master and His will; recognizing that prayer is real conversation with the invisible God; and being specific in prayer.

Prayer Is an Art

Although prayer is an art which only the Holy Spirit can teach us, I think it's important to pray until you know how to pray. Pray to be helped in prayer. Prayer is not something we can learn through reading a book. It is a discipline. It is an art, and it is hard work.

Have you ever wondered how it is that people spend thousands, even millions of dollars on paintings by the masters? Have you ever scratched your head and thought that people who stand for hours in front of a Monet are a little bit strange? Have you ever looked at a modern sculpture and thought, *I'm missing something here.* . . . Have you ever wondered why an Ansel Adams photograph can speak volumes? What do people see in art, anyway?

Perhaps you're more mystified by music. Does it seem strange to you that some people spend hundreds of dollars to buy season tickets to a symphony? That they can sit and listen for hours to a Mendelssohn concerto? Aren't they going a little bit overboard?

I remember when I had a "ho-hum" attitude toward art. I used to look at certain sculptures and snicker. I would visit museums and see people standing for long periods of time in front of paintings, and I knew I was somehow missing the point.

But my attitude began to change when I met my art teacher. Before I even picked up my brush in our daily art lessons, we would spend an hour looking through art books. My art teacher would pause at a print by Monet, and we'd discuss the color and composition. He would flip the page, and we'd look at prints by Cézanne or Gauguin. We'd discuss color tests, the experiments, the values of light and dark, the hues of the various shades of pink and blue.

At first I felt . . . well, bored. But the more I looked and listened, the more I began to appreciate. Spending time with those masters, page after page, began to elevate my thinking. The more I looked at works of art, the more frequently I visited museums. The more I visited museums, the more that was revealed. The more that was revealed, the more I understood. The more I understood, the more I felt joy. Now when I see people studying a Rembrandt, I understand what they are appreciating. The key is this: If you don't appreciate good art, then spend time looking at good art. If you don't appreciate good music, spend long hours listening to good music.

I know people who have a similar struggle when they look at the prayer habits of others. They listen to someone who's excited about spending a morning talking to the Lord, and they

---

"Prayer is very much like other disciplines. Like art and music, it is a discipline that can only be appreciated when you actually spend time in it."

---

scratch their heads and yawn and think, *Well that's fine for them, but I just don't get it. I just don't see why they enjoy praying—maybe I'm missing something.*

Ever feel that way? Perhaps you could never imagine yourself as a "prayer warrior." You think certain people must be better equipped, maybe they're better trained, or their personalities lend themselves to prayer better than yours does. But frankly, the only way you and I can develop a real appreciation for prayer is to pray. Prayer itself is an art which only the Holy Spirit can teach.

Pray for prayer.

Pray to be helped in prayer.

Pray until you appreciate prayer.

Prayer is very much like other disciplines. Like art and music, it is a discipline that can only be appreciated when you actually spend time in it. Spending time with the Master will elevate your thinking. The more you pray, the more will be revealed. You will understand. You will smile and nod your head as you identify with others who fight long battles and find great joy on their knees.

We can't afford to neglect the discipline of prayer, no more than a soldier can afford to take a vacation from boot camp.

The more you pray, the more you will be like Abraham, who felt as though he was dust and ashes. You will be like Jacob, who said, "I will not let Thee go until Thou bless me." You will be prepared to face what lies ahead in life.

The more you pray, the more you will understand, the more joy you will have, and the more you will know the greatness of our God.

Prayer Point

If you are earnest about seeking God, you should be earnest about prayer. Take a moment now to pray. Put this book down, close your eyes, still your heart, and quiet your thoughts. Think about dust and ashes.

Kneel before God in your imagination on the floor of the throne room. Approach with awe and reverence and a holy kind of carefulness. God is very real, and we should be humbled that He delights in hearing our requests, that He welcomes our words, and that He is happy to hear what we say. But we can't take that kind of freedom for granted. We should simply lift holy hands before Him, hands made clean through the blood of Jesus Christ, and say, "Father, we praise You, we adore You, we extol You, we magnify and glorify You."

For several minutes, speak to God about speaking with God. Keep your conversation with Him specifically about prayer. Ask Him to help you pray until you can pray, until you appreciate the discipline, the art, of prayer. Ask Him to help you understand because He promises to reveal, and in so doing you will receive joy. Pray in Jesus' name, and thank Him for welcoming you into His family. Praise God for Jesus and for listening to

your prayer because of Jesus. Thank Him for your spiritual journey and the path that He has prepared for you.

For Group Discussion

1. What talent have you worked hard at developing?

2. In what ways is prayer like art and music?

3. What hard work is involved in praying? What must you practice?

4. From what you've read so far, what is a prayer warrior? What keeps you from being a prayer warrior?

5. What would you have to do to become more disciplined in praying?

Part Two

Walking the Path
Of Prayer

Seven

Seeking to Offer An Argument

> Do not reckon you have prayed unless you have pleaded, for pleading is the very marrow of prayer.
>
> CHARLES HADDON SPURGEON

I love words. I think it's fascinating to find out the meaning and origin of a word.

Consider the word *argument.* Most of us immediately think of a quarrel, don't we? We imagine a rousing ruckus where two angry people spew forth a torrent of hot, biting words, eventually ending up throwing things around the room.

But *argument,* from a root word meaning "to make clear or to reason," is partially defined by Webster's dictionary as "a proof or rebuttal, a coherent series of reasons offered." In other words, to argue is to offer reasons, to give evidence. When people argue, they offer proofs supporting their convictions.

Argument, then, is rather a good word!

When you think about it, there are many stories in the Bible of great men of faith arguing with the Lord. Job argued before God, but he did not quarrel. Anger had nothing to do with his argument. He simply desired to present himself and his convictions before the Lord.

Don't Argue in Anger

Marriage has taught me a lot about the meaning of the word *argument*. I've been married almost ten years, and I don't pretend to be an expert on marriage, but with my disability my husband and I have learned a lot about how to argue.

It's inevitable that a marriage partner is going to get angry. At some point, someone in the marriage is going to get their feelings bruised over unmet expectations or inevitable misunderstandings. Anger will raise its stubborn head. Now anger itself is not a sin, but the Bible makes it clear that we had better handle anger properly so that we don't sin.

The worst way to handle anger is to quarrel. Quarreling, unlike arguing, is an explosive shouting match, a hot-tempered contest to see which one of you can throw the biggest barbs. I know that when I have quarreled I have felt as though I were reading a bad script: "You never do this!" "You always do that!" "It really makes me mad when you . . ." Sound familiar?

Quarreling is the wrong way to handle anger. Instead, God would have us argue.

Arguing Wisely

When my husband and I argue, I have to admit that Ken is a fair fighter. He can usually get angry without getting destructive. He fights—but he fights fair.

Except, the other night he pulled a fast one. We were arguing in the living room, and our discussion was going rather smoothly—for an argument, that is. But his temper got a little hot when I let some stupid remark slip. That did it. Ken stomped out of the living room and slammed the door. Do you know what that meant? I was unable to follow him. I physically could not open the living room door to follow him into the kitchen. I was stuck.

To me, that was fighting unfairly. Well, I put a lid on my own temper, lowered my voice, and politely reminded Ken that shutting doors was a low blow. With that, the living room door slowly cracked open, and I was able to wheel into the kitchen where, I'm glad to tell you, our silly argument was resolved.

Fighting fair? It's essential if you and your spouse—or your friend or roommate—are going to be able not only to air your

---

"Quarreling is the wrong way to handle anger. Instead, God would have us argue."

---

differences but honestly deal with them. And it's a good principle to remember when approaching God with our reasons and convictions. In other words, there are rules for presenting a good argument.

First, remember to *argue*, not quarrel. When Ken and I argue, we first bite our tongues, then we sit down and begin to reason. I have to promise to listen with an open heart and an open mind for an entire fifteen minutes. I can't interrupt. I can't interject. I can't defend myself. I promise to listen, knowing that after fifteen minutes, Ken will be quiet and I will get to share my point of view. That's when I have an opportunity to share my case, give good reasons, and point to the evidence.

Back and forth we go until we resolve the conflict.

My wheelchair has helped us learn how to handle our anger properly. I can't stomp out of the house, slam the door, or get in the car and roar down the street to a friend's house. It's not as though I can lock the bedroom door and go to bed early, pull the covers over my head, and turn my back on my husband in disgust. About the worst thing I can do to my husband is run over his toes!

So I hope you can understand how we relate to what Paul wrote in 2 Corinthians 12:9–10: "Therefore I will boast all the more gladly about my weaknesses, so that Christ's power may rest on me. That is why, for Christ's sake, I delight in weaknesses, in insults, in hardships, in persecutions, in difficulties. For when I am weak, then I am strong."

My wheelchair is an asset to us rather than a liability. If anything, it has taught us how to argue.

Giving God Your Reasons

To argue, then, is to offer reasons or to give evidence. When someone argues, he puts forth proofs of his convictions. Do you remember what Job said? "If only I knew where to find him; if only I could go to his dwelling! I would state my case before him and fill my mouth with arguments" (Job 23:3–4).

If you believe strongly enough about a concern that you would bring it before God in prayer, be prepared to offer an argument, a reason why you feel the Lord would be glorified through your request. Fill your mouth with a good case statement, not flattery or fancy phrases or pat petitions you may have said scores of times before. To argue is to take the time and thought to offer reasons to God.

I admire "argumentative" prayer. I think God is pleased to listen to someone who takes his prayer seriously enough to contend for what he believes. Remember, God said to Isaiah, "Come now, let us reason together" (Isaiah 1:18).

God asks us to plead with Him, to seriously weigh our words when we come into His presence, to bring forth our pros and cons, to put deep thought into our prayer. As Spurgeon said, "When a man searches arguments for a thing, it is because he attaches importance to that which he is seeking." And God loves a man who will converse with Him like that.

But why should we argue at all? Well, it's obviously not because God needs to be informed. He knows the reasons for our

---

"I admire 'argumentative' prayer. I think God is pleased to listen to someone who takes his prayer seriously enough to contend for what he believes."

---

circumstances, and He knows more about our situation than we do. There is nothing we could tell God that He doesn't already know. We don't argue because God is lacking information. We don't argue because He is slow to give and has to be pushed and prodded to do His will. No. We argue not for His benefit but for ours.

We are to involve ourselves in our prayers, to test our thoughts in order to see if a thing is truly of the Lord and His will. To paraphrase it, God inasmuch said to Isaiah, "Come now, put on your thinking cap and let's reason this thing out *together.*" The Lord delights in having His children come to Him that way. God wants us to involve ourselves in prayer. He wants us not simply to talk to Him but to converse with Him.

The Lord tells you to come and reason with Him. God issued the invitation to Isaiah, and He extends the same invitation to you today.

Seeking Answers for Our Questions

A few years ago I was in Grand Rapids, Michigan, for a bookstore party. I had just finished my book, *Choices . . . Changes,* and my publisher wanted me to come to the city to meet and talk with the sales representatives. That also meant visiting a local bookstore to help promote my new work.

At the bookstore party there was a long line of people waiting for me to autograph their books. Autographs are frustrating for me because I'd rather be talking than signing my name—you see, I have to write with a pen between my teeth, and I can't talk to people and write at the same time.

Anyway, in the long line there stood a girl about ten years old. She was clutching a tattered copy of my first book, *Joni*. In a shy voice she said, "My name is Kitty. I read this when I was a little girl. It means a lot to me because I have a heart disease, and I can't go out and play with my friends. And Joni, I don't know . . . I've got a lot of questions for God."

At that point it was all I could do not to cry. I noticed her mother patting her shoulder. I didn't have time to talk privately with Kitty's mother then, but in my heart I prayed, *Dear God, please let that mom allow her daughter to have questions.*

God Expects Questions

You see, I know when I was first injured, I was relieved the God of the Bible was not human-sized, but God-sized. And He could handle my toughest questions. It impressed me to know that God was not intimidated by my interrogation or threatened by my doubts. In fact, at times I almost sensed God saying, "Come now, Joni, let's reason together. Put your thinking cap on. Let's work this problem out."

I leaned down to Kitty and I said, "Don't be afraid of your questions. Our God is big enough to handle your biggest doubts. In fact, there was even a man in the Bible who said, 'Lord, I believe. Help my unbelief.' And, Kitty, that's what you're doing when you talk to God. You believe in Him simply because you're talking to

Him. But be honest enough to share your questions and concerns. He won't be intimidated. He'll love talking with you."

A wide-eyed look of wondrous revelation spread across Kitty's face. When she smiled, it was as though a bright light dawned

---

"I was relieved the God of the Bible was not human-sized, but God-sized. And He could handle my toughest questions. It impressed me to know that God was not intimidated by my interrogation or threatened by my doubts."

---

above her head as she realized God was not afraid of her questions. For that matter, she didn't have to be afraid of presenting her heartfelt concerns to the Lord. He knew them anyway. Why shouldn't Kitty be honest with Him and share what was on her heart? She needed to be consoled not to smother her querying, but to think through her faith until she could better understand the character of God and His response to her questions.

I can identify with Kitty. When I was first injured, my mind swirled with questions, and I turned to the book of Job for answers. I was desperate to know why and how, but I found that the book of Job raised more questions than it answered.

You see, God refused to answer Job's agonizing questions. He also declined to comment on all the tidy theological theories offered by Job's erstwhile friends. Yet Job's pointed, sharp questions continued:

Why didn't You let me die at birth? (3:11–19)

Why do You keep wretched people like me alive? (3:20–22)

How do You expect me to have hope and patience? (6:11)

You're the One who created me, so why are You destroying me? (10:8–9)

Why do You hide Your face and consider me Your enemy? (13:24)

Job's friends were horrified. They probably expected lightning to fall and fry poor, suffering Job on the spot. But the lightning never fell. And that, to me, demonstrates that God did not condemn Job for his doubt and despair. God was ready to take on his hard questions. And the answers? They came, but they weren't the ones Job was expecting.

I drew comfort from that. I was consoled to know that God did not condemn me for putting Him under the interrogation lamp. I didn't have to worry about offending God by my outbursts in times of fear and pain. My despair wasn't going to shock Him. God, according to the book of Job, cannot be threatened by questions from Job . . . or Joni . . . or Kitty . . . or you. God can handle any question you have.

The next time you find yourself in a perplexing situation that demands prayer, discuss with God how you think He might be glorified in the situation. Present to Him the reasons you think He should move or act out His will. Tell Him how you believe His kingdom will be advanced, His people encouraged, His Word honored. Let Him know that you have searched to find His heart. Let Him know that you want to plead with Him and, in so doing, let Him see that you are attaching great importance to the request you are presenting before His throne. And don't forget to argue fairly—keep your mind open for change and be sure to listen to Him. After all, God will have a thing or two to say to you in this argument!

Prayer Point

Think of a request or an intercession you have recently brought before the Lord in prayer. It could be something as simple as:

"Lord, will You please bring a helper into the life of my neighbor with a disability. She has so many needs and can't go it alone."

Now, list five good reasons for your request. They could include:

1. Lord, You were compassionate toward disabled people when You walked on earth and You met their needs. Please meet the needs of my friend that way.

2. Lord, You promised to feed the ravens and clothe the flowers of the field. My disabled neighbor has basic needs like that, and You care much more for her than You do for the birds and flowers.

3. Lord, my neighbor is in need of seeing and feeling Your personal care. A helper—even a Christian helper—could be Your "hands" to her.

4. Lord, You cared about "the least of the brethren," and my disabled neighbor certainly qualifies under that category! Please meet her need as an evidence of Your concern for the least of the brethren.

5. Lord, the rest of my neighbors will be inspired and encouraged to help, and they may even "know we are Christians by our love for one another."

Got the picture? Get out a pencil, a pad of paper, and your Bible, and list your own five reasons for that special request God has laid on your heart.

For Group Discussion

1. What's good and what's bad about arguments?

2. When do you feel like arguing with God? How can these arguments improve your prayer?

3. How are talking, conversing, arguing, and praying different from each other?

4. Why is it helpful to support your prayers with reasons?

5. How might stating reasons for your requests affect the
way you pray?

Eight

Seeking God Through His Attributes

> You and I may take hold at any time upon the
> justice and the mercy and the faithfulness and
> the wisdom, the longsuffering and the tender-
> ness of God, and we shall find there every at-
> tribute of the Most High to be, as it were, a
> great battering ram with which we may open
> the gates of heaven.
>
> CHARLES HADDON SPURGEON

I love Spurgeon's attitude! Now, I'm sure he wasn't saying the gates of heaven were ever closed to his prayer, but that the attributes of God give us a unique power in prayer. A higher dimension in prayer becomes open to us when we fill up our praises, intercessions, and petitions with His attributes.

Reminding Ourselves of God's Character

God enjoys it when we consciously seek His glory, His will, His character, and His heart in every situation. Consider the story of Abraham. When that old patriarch presented his case before God, he reminded the Lord, "Will not the Judge of all the earth do right?" (Genesis 18:25). Obviously God did not need to be reminded of His own justice. Abraham's prayer was persuasive because he pleaded, using God's character. In a small way, I understand what Abraham was doing when he took hold of God and reminded Him of His justice.

In the early days of my paralysis, part of my depression had to do with my fears over a bleak and hopeless future. Would I ever smile again? Would my life have meaning? Could anything good come from useless hands and feet? My depression was eased when a friend showed me a promise in the Bible about God's attribute of faithfulness. Philippians 1:6 told me to be confident that "He who began a good work in you will carry it on to completion until the day of Christ Jesus."

My friend said, "Joni, why don't you use that verse as a kind of 'lever.' Hold God to His Word. Believe He began a good work in you long before your accident. Why don't you contend, in prayer, that He will carry out that good work even though you're in a wheelchair?"

What my friend said made sense; I realized my passport out of depression would be the faithfulness of God. Taking a grip on His tenderness and mercy, I quoted Philippians 1:6 back to the Lord time and again. Obviously, God needed no reminder of His faithfulness, but frankly, I believe He was delighted with my prayer. He enjoyed the fact that I took my prayer seriously, that I was ready to argue His faithfulness with Him and say, "Lord, You're the One who wrote that verse in Philippians, and I'm holding You to it. I know You're a promise-keeper because You say in Psalm 89 that You will never betray Your faithfulness. So I can say confidently that this is Your will: Carry to completion the good things You began in my life before my diving accident."

Being able to pray that way was a breath of fresh air. And you know what? I found peace. My depression was lifted. God was being faithful; He was keeping His promise.

He Continues a Good Work

Oh, what a difference that prayer made. It was as though God pushed the fast-forward button on my walk with Him, and I began growing, as they say, by leaps and bounds. Out of no-

---

"God enjoys it when we consciously seek His glory, His will, His character, and His heart in every situation."

---

where, I began thirsting for His Word. Surprisingly, I was hungering after His righteousness. I began to see God "carrying to completion" His Son's life in me. My changed life, which was full of peace, patience, and joy, was a miraculous result of that simple prayer in which I pleaded the faithfulness of God.

Now what if I had not prayed that prayer? What if I had not been bold enough to remind God of His faithfulness to Philippians 1:6? Would the Lord have continued to carry out His good work in me? Sure, He would have—He's faithful to His promises whether I remind Him of them or not!

But here's the point. I believe a special bond, a forged closeness, was custom-made between the Lord and me during those times of pleading in prayer. And who knows? Perhaps my life may not have changed as dramatically had I not spoken that prayer. Maybe God even speeded up the process!

He Continues a Good Work in You

I can imagine your thoughts: *This chapter is making me feel guilty. I can't pray that way. . . . I don't know enough Scripture to fill one sentence of a prayer. I'm too timid to pray using*

God's attributes anyway. I guess I've just never seen the Lord work that way with me.

If I've described you, if you think God will not "carry to completion" the good work He's begun in your life, then take comfort from this story:

Several years ago I was asked to record an album of songs. To get an idea of how the recording was done, I went down to the studio several days in advance just to listen to the rest of the musicians lay down the orchestral background music. Gathered in the little studio were some of the best musicians in Los Angeles: violinists and percussionists, guitar players, piano players, and all the rest.

When the arranger handed out the scores for a tune, these professionals would glance at it, rehearse it once, and go for a "take" to actually record. I was amazed they could play a very complicated score on sight. Most amazing of all, their efforts resulted in absolutely beautiful music.

But I was overwhelmed by what happened next. When the engineers in the booth played back the finished product, most of the expert musicians actually left the room! They took a break and milled around outside, sipping Cokes or coffee, oblivious to the beauty of the music they had just helped create. I couldn't believe it! How could they walk away and not want to hear how lovely the song sounded in its final form?

The musicians' interest in the music was dulled because they had recorded hundreds of other songs. What was so special about these? They did their jobs well, and they were finished.

Unlike those musicians, God doesn't walk away from His creation. Even though He has worked in thousands of lives, He doesn't take a break from His work in you. He's creating something beautiful in you, something far more lovely than a symphony of sound. For Him, it's not simply another job that needs to be done. His reputation is at stake and His Son's image is the model. It's perfection that God has in mind—maturity in Christ is the end result He seeks.

So please don't be fainthearted, thinking that your prayer life will never advance so far as to "plead the attributes of God." Don't give up . . . and don't think God gives up on you. He wants to carry

---

"God doesn't walk away from His creation. . . . He doesn't take a break from His work in you. He's creating something beautiful in you, . . . His reputation is at stake and His Son's image is the model. It's perfection that God has in mind—maturity in Christ is the end result He seeks."

---

to completion the work of prayer He has begun in your life. He's going to be around all the way until the day of Jesus Christ—to hear and see the dramatic impact of your prayers.

Confidently Claim God's Attributes

Since God is so concerned with what He's doing in your life, you can confidently hold Him to His Word and claim His attributes in prayer. David did that. Discouraged by his own sins and unfaithfulness, he cried unto the Lord:

"Remember, O LORD, your great mercy and love, for they are from of old. Remember not the sins of my youth and my rebellious ways; according to your love remember me, for you are good, O LORD" (Psalm 25:6–7).

Does it sound a little cheeky to remind God of His attributes? Of His promises? Does it seem presumptuous? Yes, if you're the timid type. But remember, the Lord wants you to grow in prayer—yes, even becoming a bold warrior in prayer.

How about it? Would you involve God in your prayer? If you're hurting or confused, find one of God's great attributes and, as Spurgeon says, use it "as . . . a great battering ram with which we may open the gates of heaven." Claim His love, plead His holiness, remind Him of His goodness, recount His long-suffering, present to Him His power, and pray His steadfastness. If remorseful and repentant over your sin, remind Him of His tender mercies. If you're in confusion, read to Him His own words about wisdom from Proverbs 4. If you're praying for your child, present your petition before the Lord, recounting to Him stories of how He blessed little children and delighted in them.

One final thought. The more you center in prayer on God's attributes, the more those attributes become a part of your life. Focus on God's mercies, and you will become merciful. Plead with Him His wisdom, and wisdom will be yours. Center your thoughts on His holiness, and you will grow in holiness. "But we all, with open face beholding as in a glass the glory of the Lord, are changed into the same image from glory to glory, even as by the Spirit of the Lord" (2 Corinthians 3:18, KJV).

Grab on to an attribute of God with all your heart and ask Him to deal with you accordingly. Humbly hold Him to His promises. God is delighted when you seek His will, His character, His glory—and yes, His heart—in your prayers.

Prayer Point

Let's pause and enjoy God's attributes! Pray with me, saying:

> My God, infinite is Thy might, boundless Thy love, limitless Thy grace, glorious Thy saving name. I ask great things of a great God. You are known, but beyond knowledge, revealed but unrevealed. You are the almighty Instructor; possess our minds with the grandeur

of Thy perfections. Let us never forget Thy patience, wisdom, power, faithfulness, care, and never cease to respond to Thy invitations. (Valley of Vision, *a collection of Puritan prayers and devotions*)

For Group Discussion

1. What attributes of God can you name off the top of your head?

2. Of all God's attributes, which ones do you depend on the most?

3. What is your favorite attribute of God? How does it fit into your prayer life?

4. How can remembering God's faithfulness help you during difficult circumstances?

5. How can God's attributes be used like a great battering ram in prayer?

6. What should you do to become bolder in prayer?

Nine

Seeking God Through His Promises

The sacred promises, though in themselves most sure and precious, are of no avail for the comfort and sustenance of the soul unless you grasp them by faith, plead them in prayer, expect them by hope, and receive them with gratitude.

CHARLES HADDON SPURGEON

God is looking for men and women who will prove Him and His Word. There are no loopholes in His promises, and He delights in finding those people who will confirm the good things about His name and His Word through their suffering. God's promises are like a "crowbar to pry open" the storehouse of His grace.

In a way, God has given me the chance to do just that from this wheelchair. Twenty-five years have passed since my diving accident, and I've had a few years of practice trying God's Word and proving His goodness and grace. If I were to sum it up, I would join with the psalmist in saying, "Your promises have been thoroughly tested, and your servant loves them" (Psalm 119:140).

What a change in attitude for me! There was a time when God's Word seemed burdensome. I could barely bring myself to give thanks in all things. It was drudgery to think that His grace was sufficient . . . if, indeed, that meant experiencing His grace from a wheelchair. It was hard to visualize how all things could possibly fit together into a pattern for good when I could not see any good in hands that were useless and legs that could not walk.

But now I hang Psalm 119:140 over my desk. I love God's promises because I have seen His Word work, and I have confidence His promises will see me through a lot more in the future.

It was through the trial of a broken neck that God proved in my life Romans 8:28: "And we know that in all things God works for the good of those who love him, who have been called according to his purpose." And His purpose is . . . making me more like Jesus. And that's good!

Think of it. Can you be one of those people through whom God delights to prove His promises? Have you viewed your suffering, however great or small, as a testing ground of Bible promises? If you have, I hope your heart will join with mine in saying, "Your promises have been thoroughly tested and Your servant loves them."

Plead God's Promises with Certainty

We can plead God's promises with certainty. There's no need to doubt or second-guess when you pray. There's no need to scratch your head, unsure of what you're talking about. You can be *certain* of God's promises. It is this which will give you certainty in prayer.

For instance, look at Solomon's prayer of dedication for the temple of Israel:

"O LORD, God of Israel, there is no God like you in heaven. . . . Now LORD, God of Israel, keep for your servant David my father the promises you made to him when you said, 'You shall never fail to have a man to sit before me on the throne of Israel, if only your sons are careful in all they do to walk before me as you have done.' And now, O God of Israel, let your word that you promised your servant David my father come true." (1 Kings 8:23–26)

Talk about being certain in prayer! Solomon had obviously made a spiritual diary of God's promises—the ones the Lord

---

"We can plead God's promises with certainty. There's no need to doubt or second-guess when you pray."

---

had given to David, his father—and took God at His word of honor. And don't you think God was delighted to fulfill that great promise in front of Solomon and His people?

The Bible is replete with God's pledges and oaths, His vows and words of honor. And most of those promises God has given to you! Of course He would want you to be certain in prayer as you present to Him those promises.

You Can Trust God

Do not be anxious about anything, but in everything, by prayer and petition, with thanksgiving, present your requests to God. And the peace of God, which transcends all understanding, will guard your hearts and your minds in Christ Jesus. (Philippians 4:6–7)

Four or five years after my accident, I was piecing together the puzzle of my suffering by delving and digging into God's Word. As a result, the Lord began to increase the capacity of my heart for Himself. The depression I had known simply vanished.

Sure, I had occasional setbacks of despondency and discouragement, but for the most part, I knew I was progressing in my journey toward knowing God.

I could definitely see progress when I began to pray God's promises. Let me explain.

My family and I, years ago, took a month-long camping trip to Canada. We rented a Winnebago and drove deep into the province of Alberta, a beautiful part of the Rocky Mountains. We drove by glacier-scarred peaks, turquoise-blue rivers, broad alpine valleys; I sat by an open window, drinking in the sweet, crisp smell of pine air. I loved it!

We set up camp at Whistler's Mountain near Jasper, Alberta. Now, my family is the hardy, outdoor type. They love to hike, ride horses, and play tennis. So it didn't surprise me when Mom, Dad, and my sisters wanted to hike up the path to the towering cliffs above camp. "I'll remain behind," I said. I didn't want them to feel guilty about leaving me. I was as excited for them as if I were going myself. I would stay by the tent, read a book, and wait around until they returned.

After they threw on their backpacks, I watched them trek up the path. I was happy for them, but I had mixed emotions. I found it difficult to sit there, and soon I felt tears welling up. I'm sure I could have used that time for a mountain-sized pity party, but instead, I decided to put the matter to prayer. I brought before God a promise of which I was certain.

I spoke aloud the gist of Philippians 4:6, "Be anxious about nothing, but present your requests to God and the peace of God will keep your heart and mind in Jesus," and I began to pray. I said, "Lord, I know it is Your will for people to enjoy Your creation. That's why You've given us this beauty—the mountains, the trees, the streams. And Lord, I'm thankful for how beautiful and refreshing it all is to my heart. But God, I know You understand that I am human—You know all about my feelings right now.

"And so, as You told me to do in Philippians 4, I want to present my request to You: Please bring Your creation close to me, God. I can't get out into it, that's obvious, but I'm asking You to put me in touch with Your creation in a special way. And as You do, I take You at Your promise. . . . I believe You'll give me peace which transcends all understanding."

I offered that prayer, but I wasn't certain what avenue the Lord would take to answer it. I thought perhaps He would have a butterfly flit across my path or a caterpillar crawl across my knee. Anything to remind me of His presence and the closeness of His creation would have been fine.

Minutes passed—an hour in fact—and my interest returned to my book. Before long, my prayer slipped my mind. My family returned from their hiking trip, and as they slung off their backpacks, they told me all about their hike.

An Unexpected Answer to Prayer

That night after dinner, my sister Kathy, my dad, and I sat around the campfire singing hymns. "Trust and obey, for there's no other

---

"You, too, can plead God's promises with certainty. Take God at His word. Believe His promises. Expect a great answer to prayer."

---

way . . . ," we were harmonizing and having a good time. As we sang, though, I looked behind my sister, who was sitting across from me, and I saw what looked like a big black dog.

"Kathy, you'd better stop singing. There's something behind you."

She ignored me and started on the second verse.

"Wait a minute, that isn't a dog—it's a black bear! Kathy," I whispered hoarsely, "stop singing! There's a bear behind you!"

She just kept singing. "Trust and obey . . ."

"Kathy, stop singing! A bear is breathing down your neck!"

"There's no bear behind me," she laughed, but she stopped singing and turned around. Kathy and the bear locked eyes, then she froze, paralyzed with fear and excitement.

We sat very still and watched as the bear sniffed around Kathy's log, ambled over to me, and then sniffed my wheelchair. He smelled my foot pedals! He was sniffing the cuff of my jeans! I was so terrified, yet thrilled.

My sister Jay, who was in the Winnebago washing dishes, heard the commotion, so she threw open the camper door and exclaimed, "Bear? Where?"

That panicked the bear. He whirled around, upset the Coleman stove, pots and pans, banged the picnic table, and galloped off into the night. My sisters scrambled for their cameras and ran after him.

As I lay in bed that night, I thought, *Wow, what a first-class answer to prayer!* This was no little butterfly or caterpillar. It was almost as if God, with His marvelous sense of humor, said, "You want to get closer to My creation? I'll get you so close to My creation, you'll never want to be that close again!"

The Lord had a reason for answering my prayer in such a big way. First, I'm sure He wanted to give me the peace He promised in Philippians 4:6—the verse I quoted to Him. But secondly, I believe God wanted to underscore a lesson. It was as if He said, "Now look, Joni, if I care enough about you to answer such a little request as, 'Bring Your creation close to me,' don't you think I am deeply concerned about the intimate details of your life that really matter? The loneliness, the heartache, the feelings of inferiority?"

As I lay in bed, I was filled with indescribable peace. The peace God had promised.

You, too, can plead God's promises with certainty. Take God at His word. Believe His promises. Expect a great answer to prayer. God may not bring a bear to your front door, but the next time you present to God one of His promises, expect Him to keep it.

Prayer Point

People rely on different promises at different times. Select one of these to pray today:

- A promise for peace: "You will keep him in perfect peace, whose mind is stayed on You, because he trusts in You." (Isaiah 26:3, NKJV)

- A promise for when you're depressed: "Therefore humble yourselves under the mighty hand of God, that He may exalt you in due time, casting all your care upon Him, for He cares for you." (1 Peter 5:6–7, NKJV)

- A promise for when you're tempted: "For in that He Himself has suffered, being tempted, He is able to aid those who are tempted." (Hebrews 2:18, NKJV)

- A promise for when you're impatient: "I waited patiently for the LORD; and He inclined to me, and heard my cry." (Psalm 40:1, NKJV)

- A promise for when you're hurting: "Wait on the LORD; be of good courage, and He shall strengthen your heart; wait, I say, on the LORD!" (Psalm 27:14, NKJV)

For Group Discussion

1. When did someone disappoint you because he or she did not keep a promise?

2. How do we know that God always keeps His promises?

3. How has God proven His faithfulness to you in the past? How does knowing that God is faithful affect the way you pray and live?

4. What particular promise in the Bible has been especially meaningful to you? How has it helped you?

5. How should the fact that God always keeps His promises change the way you pray from now on?

Ten

Seeking God Through The Power of His Name

Through the Spirit of holiness . . . declared
with power to be the Son of God by his resurrection from the dead: Jesus Christ our Lord.
Through him and for his name's sake, we received grace. . . .

ROMANS 1:4–5

W hat's in a name? Sometimes, everything.
The most powerful word we could ever say in prayer is
the name of Jesus. Charles Spurgeon said it this way: "The man
of God's plea is not his own merit, but the Name. The saints
have always felt this to be their most mighty plea. God Himself
has performed His grandest deeds of grace for the honor of His
Name, and His people know that this is the most potent argument with Him."

We often invoke the name of our Lord when we pray, un-
aware of how powerful His name really is. The name of Christ
saves (1 John 2:2). The name of Christ protects (Zechariah 2:5).
The name of Christ gives guidance (Isaiah 9:6). The name of
Christ delivers (Romans 11:26).

Andrew Murray said, "The name of Christ is the expression
of everything He has done and everything He is and lives to do

as our Mediator." So when we pray in Jesus' name, we are using that word which represents Jesus to us and to the Father—we are bringing before God our requests as voiced through the honor, power, and kingdom of Jesus.

The Father hears and answers those kinds of prayers . . . and He answers them in a powerful way.

For His Name's Sake

I love wheeling into my art studio and splashing around my acrylics and watercolors. In the past, I've also sketched a lot of charcoal and pastel pencil renderings. To be a good painter, an artist must be thoroughly skilled in the basics, such as drawing life figures.

Early in my art career, I took classes in life drawing; that is, studying the uncovered human figure. Any good art instructor will tell you it's essential, if you're going to paint people, to understand skeletal structure and muscles, and how they fit together—how the leg joins at the hip when a woman is sitting, or how a man's torso appears when he is doubled over is key to painting human figures in action. Life drawing is part of the discipline of a serious artist.

I've never shared this in print before, but a few years ago I did a series of nudes. Looking back though, I'm afraid I pushed the forms a bit too far. Perhaps because I was struggling with my own self-image, the nude figures were rather voluptuous. But they were good drawings, and I was pleased with them.

Like all of my other drawings, I signed my sketches of the nude figure "Joni, PTL" (Praise the Lord), because I wanted to give God credit where credit was due. My heart motive was honestly pure. In fact, I was so thrilled, I had those drawings framed for exhibition.

During one of my first art exhibits there were five nudes shown and all of them sold. Four went to close family and friends, and one went to a stranger, a lady in Pennsylvania.

"The most powerful word we could ever say in prayer is the name of Jesus."

Second Thoughts

Two years later, when I was beginning work on my first book, *Joni*, I remembered that nude painting. *Hmm. I wonder where that painting is. I can just see what might happen. I'll be on some television show talking about my artwork, and someone will bring up that sensual-looking nude with "Joni PTL" plastered all over it. Who has that nude, and what are they using it for?*

I shuddered to think how this might possibly damage my testimony for the Lord Jesus simply because someone might not understand the motives for which the nude was drawn. I was scared, but then I read, "The name of the LORD is a strong tower; the righteous run to it and are safe" (Proverbs 18:10).

So I prayed, "Lord, I don't want Your name to get tarnished. There are already enough reasons the world finds to attack Your name without Christians like me adding fuel to the fire. So God, wherever that nude is, defend Your reputation mightily. Lord, will You protect it and keep the owner from using it against You? I pray this for the sake of Your name, Your reputation, just as I offer this prayer in Your name."

I prayed in His name. The matter was settled.

Two weeks later I appeared on the "Today" show with Barbara Walters, and all my line drawings were displayed in the studio. The camera slowly panned each one, and Ms. Walters asked me what PTL meant. I explained the signature meant

"Praise the Lord"—a marvelous chance to share my testimony on national television.

Barbara Walters was kind and generous. She and her staff people helped me pack up my paintings; and my friends and I headed for the taxi, loaded up with all my artwork in the back, and drove to the New York airport to fly home to Baltimore.

Now, if you've ever been to JFK International, you know it is crazy and confusing even on a quiet day. There are dozens of terminals and countless numbers of planes. New York City traffic was bad that morning, and we rushed through the security area, late for our plane. My paintings were checked through security, and, as usual, one of the guards had to come up and pat my arms, waist, and legs to clear me.

As the guard frisked me, she gave me a curious look and asked, "Weren't you on the 'Today' show this morning?"

"Yes, I was."

"I must tell you," she went on, "a couple years ago, my mother gave me one of your beautiful paintings."

I thought she was referring to a print or reproduction, so I commented, "Oh really? Which one?"

She smiled. "My mom, who lives in Pennsylvania, bought a charcoal sketch of a nude figure from you, and my husband and I are so proud of it. We have it hanging in our bathroom. We think it's one of the best works of art we've ever seen."

I was stunned. "I can't believe it!" I cried as we rushed down the corridor to the plane. Tens of millions of people live between Baltimore and New York City . . . and God linked me up with the very person who had been on my mind!

I didn't have time to get the security guard's address or phone number, but I'll never forget her words as she waved good-bye: "We love your drawing and we'll take good care of it. We love you!"

What a powerful answer to prayer. I expected that God would, in His all-knowing way, guard that painting wherever it ended up. His good name was at stake and, in a way, my testimony in Him was on the line. I had prayed with His name in mind—but little did I realize God would introduce me to the very woman who owned the painting!

"Our capacity to believe in the power of God is linked to our knowledge of His name."

This little story reminds me that God will perform His grandest deeds of grace for the honor of His name. When we pray with a heartfelt concern for His honor, God will delight in answering our prayers, demonstrating that He guards His righteous reputation. You and I have said it a hundred times when we've quoted that favorite psalm: "He guides me in paths of righteousness *for his name's sake*" (Psalm 23:3, emphasis added).

Our capacity to believe in the power of God is linked to our knowledge of His name. The psalmist said, "Those who know your name will trust in you" (Psalm 9:10). Victory in difficult circumstances is also linked to the power of His name: "Through you we push back our enemies; through your name we trample our foes" (Psalm 44:5).

We have boldness before God in prayer . . . yet only in the name of Jesus. We have power over the spiritual forces of darkness in prayer . . . yet only because of His name. We have authority to intervene in the affairs of men through our prayers . . . yet only if we humbly invoke the authority of Jesus Christ our Lord, the Name above all names.

Your life will have power, your prayers will be powerful if you live and speak in the name of your Lord.

Prayer Point

The name of Christ has power. You may feel weakness in prayer, but the fact is, when you pray in the name of Jesus, your intercessions and petitions have potency before the Father.

Sometimes it's good to sing your prayer! Take the words of this favorite song and make them a prayer, praising the Lord for His great name:

> O Lord, our Lord, how majestic
>   is Your name in all the earth.
> O Lord, our Lord, how majestic
>   is Your name in all the earth.
> O Lord, we praise Your name.
>   O Lord, we magnify Your name:
> Prince of Peace, mighty God;
>   O Lord God Almighty.

For Group Discussion

1. Who are the most powerful people in the world?

2. When do you feel powerless? What power does Christ have over this situation?

3. How would you explain to a child why you close prayers in Jesus' name?

4. How can you claim Christ's authority in prayer?

5. What can give us boldness in our prayers? How can timid people pray boldly?

Eleven

Seeking God When Words Aren't Enough

> When thou prayest, rather let thy heart be
> without words than thy words without heart.
>
> JOHN BUNYAN

I t's not often I'm at a loss for words. But when I received a letter from a man named Steve and read his incredible story, I was stunned. Steve, a narcotics agent, was paralyzed when shot in the neck four years earlier while on duty. He wrote, "I'm having a terrible time adjusting to my situation, and some words of inspiration would really come in handy right now."

I knew I had to telephone Steve and at least make an effort to share some words of encouragement he so desperately needed. On the phone, I realized Steve was breathing with the aid of a ventilator. He'd say a few words, then pause as his respirator pulled in air. He would then quickly finish his sentence, stopping again for another breath.

I've talked with lots of ventilator quadriplegics like Steve, and I don't find a respirator distracting, but I couldn't help but think, *No wonder this guy is having a terrible time adjusting. He's lost so much.*

I was at a loss for words. And I told Steve so. We agreed, though, that sometimes words aren't needed. He understood that, in a small way, I knew what he was going through. Before we hung up, I prayed with him. He was looking forward to an operation for a nerve implant in his neck so that he could at least breathe on his own. But even after that operation, he'll still have struggles. As he said in his letter, "Just existing is a hassle."

I'm touched that Steve understood my loss for words. Finding honest, concrete words of encouragement is impossible at times. But when I reread his letter, I thought of those words from Romans: "In the same way, the Spirit helps us in our weakness. We do not know what we ought to pray, but the Spirit himself intercedes for us with groans that words cannot express" (Romans 8:26).

Pain Too Deep for Words

Hurt, sometimes, goes almost too deep. Depression grips your emotions. Fear locks your thoughts. You can't put two ideas together. You've felt that way.

At those times I'm so relieved God can read my heart. He can know what's in the deepest recesses of Steve's being. God can reach down and wrap His love around your hurting heart even when you're handicapped by your own weakness for words.

Hebrews 4:13 describes it this way: "*Nothing* in all creation is hidden from God's sight. Everything is uncovered and laid bare before the eyes of him to whom we must give account (emphasis added)."

When you and I are in such agony that we can't even express it, isn't it comforting to know God lives that agony with us? His hand is on the pulse of your hurting heart, sensitive to the faintest flutter of emotion. That is just how tender God is toward Steve right now. And that's how God hears you in your weakness. No matter what you're going through, God not only knows, He cares and is already planning how best to heal and help.

> "God can reach down and wrap His love
> around your hurting heart even when
> you're handicapped by your own
> weakness for words."

God Will Help You Pray

Nobody is as "in touch" with our heart's longings as God. And when we are too weak to pray for ourselves, God finds words for us.

If you haven't noticed, Charles Spurgeon is one of my favorite writers, and I like how he describes God's action in our prayers:

> It is a mark of wondrous condescension that God should not only answer our prayers when they are made, but should make our prayers for us. That the king should say to the petitioner, "Bring your case before me, and I will grant your desire," is kindness. But for him to say, "I will be your secretary. I will write out your petition for you. I will put it into proper words so that your petition shall be framed acceptably," this is goodness at its utmost stretch. But this is precisely what the Holy Ghost does for us poor, ignorant, wavering, weak men. Jesus in His agony was strengthened by an angel; you are to be helped by God Himself. Aaron and Hur held up the hands of Moses, but the Holy Ghost Himself helps your infirmities.

Like a Father, He Listens

There is nothing that moves a loving father's soul quite like his child's cry. What loving parent can resist the cry of his or her baby? In Psalm 5:1–2 David opens his prayer by saying, "Give ear to my words, O LORD, consider my sighing. Listen to my cry for help, my King and my God, for to you I pray."

Up to his ears in trouble, his heart pounding in fear, David wanted God to hear his cry.

Sound familiar to you parents? Of all people, you should understand how precious to God are the cries of His children. If your baby is upstairs in his crib and he cries, instantly you know what's wrong. You can tell from the sound of his cry whether he's grumpy, waking up, hungry, or hurt. A baby, unable to speak, can tell his parents many things simply by the sound of his cry.

Someone once said that prayer is the child's helpless cry to the Father's attentive ear. When our prayer goes up like a cry, God knows exactly what our need is. He can tell if our cry is an urgent prayer for help or a sighing prayer of discouragement. Maybe it's a heartwarming prayer of gratitude. Much like a mother or father with a child, God heeds the voice of our crying.

And remember, God does more than hear words—He reads hearts. David said, "O LORD, consider my sighing." Hearts sigh. And our Father delights in listening for those whispers of sighing which tell Him our heart needs help.

God Understands Our Groans

Not long ago when I was at a Special Olympics meet, a young woman with cerebral palsy approached me in her wheelchair. She kept groaning a certain sentence over and over. I couldn't make out her words, even after I asked her to repeat them several times. I didn't know if she was in terrible trouble or if she was just trying to describe some happy experience.

I felt helpless because I could not understand her. Finally a friend came along and helped me decipher what she was saying—the woman in the wheelchair had to go to the bathroom! I felt terrible. I hadn't been able to help her, because I could not understand. I couldn't discern the voice of her crying, the meaning behind her groaning.

Wouldn't it be awful if we couldn't make our needs known? If there were no one around to understand? Often that seems to be our predicament when we don't know how to pray. The best

---

"Nobody is as 'in touch' with our heart's longings as God. And when we are too weak to pray for ourselves, God finds words for us."

---

we're able to do is merely cry: our tears, liquid prayers. Well, we may be handicapped when it comes to expressing our groans and sighs to another person, but the One who searches hearts knows and understands. Our groans have a voice before God.

When We Don't Know How to Pray for Others

Our ministry at *Joni and Friends* is an outreach to those with disabilities, such as cerebral palsy, mental retardation, spinal cord injuries, muscular dystrophy, or multiple sclerosis. When I pray for these people, I remind God of the way Christ's heart was touched with compassion, not pity, when He met blind persons. When He met those who were deaf or paralyzed, He was moved with love.

I'm sure many of these people were unable to put into words all that they felt when they met the Lord Jesus. But He ministered to each unspoken request; He touched them with His love even when they didn't say a word.

And that's exactly how I prayed for Steve, my ventilator-dependent friend in a wheelchair. I may not have known how to decipher the slightest quiver in his hurting heart, but I knew that God understood; God could meet those needs.

So when I pray for the people involved with *Joni and Friends,* I remind God that people need His love now just as much as they did when Jesus walked on the earth. I plead the sorrows of God's people and remind the Father that Jesus dealt with individuals who were torn apart by heartache and loneliness. I remind the Father of Christ's compassion for those who are lost and confused. Even though I don't know the specific burdens my fellow Christians are bearing, God does.

Prayer Point

Reach back in your mind and recall the most meaningful times when a dear friend comforted you through your hurt. You may not have been able to express your heartache, but remember how your friend held you? Looked into your eyes? Cried with you? Do you recall special words that fit the need for the moment? Doesn't that memory warm your heart?

Now—transfer that remembrance to your relationship with your heavenly Father. Imagine for a moment His compassion when He hears the groaning you're too weak to even utter. Think of how instant He is in responding to your cry.

While the memory is still in your mind, talk with Him now— straight from your heart.

For Group Discussion

1. When was a time you were with someone who was hurting and you did not know what to say?

2. Why does it seem difficult to pour out your deepest feelings to God? Why is it difficult to pray when you don't know what to say?

3. How do loving parents feel when a child needs something and doesn't know how to tell them? How might this be similar to the way God listens to our hurts?

4. Knowing that God hears us and understands us when we have no words, how should we pray?

5. How might you be able to share your feelings with God when you can't put them into words?

Twelve

Seeking God In Jesus' Name

> Like others, I have prayed for healings, for miracles, for guidance, and for assistance. Frankly, there were times I was sure God would answer me because I had mustered strong feelings of faith. But many of those times nothing happened—or if it did, it was entirely unlike what I had anticipated. . . . The fact is that my prayer life cannot be directly tied to the results I expect or demand. I have had many opportunities by now to see that the things I want God to do in response to my prayers can be unhealthy for me. I have begun to see that worship and intercession are far more the business of aligning myself with God's purposes than asking Him to align with mine.
>
> GORDON MACDONALD

"In Jesus' name . . . be healed!"

Lying in bed, totally paralyzed, you can imagine how words like these voiced by a television preacher intrigued me. More than just being interested in the words of a faith healer, I was also interested in what the Bible had to say about healing. I desperately wanted out of my wheelchair!

When I studied the Bible, I was impressed that Jesus never passed over anyone who needed healing. He opened the eyes of the blind and the ears of the deaf and even raised up the paralyzed.

I was also impressed with a number of Scripture passages that seemed to indicate that I could ask whatever would be in God's will and Jesus would do it. A request for healing seemed consistent with His will, and one of my favorite passages was John 16:23–24: "My Father will give you whatever you ask in my name. Until now you have not asked for anything in my name. Ask and you will receive, and your joy will be complete."

So I began to pray for healing in Jesus' name. I used examples from the past of God's great provision for others. "Jesus Christ is the same yesterday and today and forever," I reminded God (Hebrews 13:8). "And Jesus healed back then. That means He can heal right now. So Lord, that You might receive glory, lift me up."

In order to show genuine faith, I called my friends on the telephone and said, "Hey, you guys, next time you see me I'm going to be standing on my feet." I even went to a couple of "faith healing" services. I was convinced that my healing was in God's plan and that He would raise me up to bring more glory to Himself. And praying it all in Jesus' name seemed to put the seal on my destiny.

But nothing happened. Days, weeks passed, and I would look at my arms and legs as though they were separate from me, and think, "You're healed, body!" For some reason, my fingers and my feet didn't get the message. My mind said, "Move!" but nothing happened.

God's Answer to Prayer

I couldn't understand. Didn't God's Word promise I could ask for anything in Jesus' name and it would be granted so that my joy would be complete? Surely God knew it would overjoy me to be healed.

I thought perhaps I wasn't searching the Scriptures thoroughly enough. It was then God led me back to Hebrews, the same book in which I found that marvelous verse about His being the same yesterday, today, and forever.

In the eleventh chapter of Hebrews, I found that roll call of great heroes of the faith—seventeen men and women who, because of their God-honoring and God-pleasing faith, experi-

---

"Surely God knew it would overjoy me to be healed. . . . [But] God had a better plan for me. I began to see my healing was not physical, but spiritual."

---

enced miracles. People like Noah, Abraham, Isaac, Jacob, Joseph, and others. These people conquered kingdoms, gained what was promised, shut the mouths of lions, escaped the edge of the sword, and received the dead back to life.

But then I noticed an interesting change initiated by two little words in verse 35: "and others." Others were tortured; some faced jeers and floggings. Others were chained and put in prison. They were stoned. These saints had just as much God-honoring and God-pleasing faith as those named earlier in the chapter—but they did not receive miracles.

I realized I was probably among those who had faith, yet also a lifetime of hard knocks and trials. I was comforted by Hebrews 11:39–40: "These were all commended for their faith, yet none of them received what had been promised. God had planned something better for us so that only together with us would they be made perfect."

God had a better plan for me. I began to see my healing was not physical, but spiritual. Through that search I learned more about God, which is really what most of His answers to prayer are about anyway. I learned that Jesus is the same yesterday, today, and forever: always just, always holy, always full of love, always sensitive, always long-suffering. He never has, and never will, change.

Praying in Jesus' Name

But what about that verse from John 16? What about praying in Jesus' name? Wasn't that a guarantee?

I suppose I used the promise, "my Father will give you whatever you ask in my name" as a carte blanche approach to prayer. I assumed it was God's will to put me back on my feet. But God's will obviously meant something bigger and, yes, even better. It's taken me years to understand, but the deep and enduring joy I have has far outlived whatever immediate joy I would have experienced had I been healed. It's all because I've finally learned what it means to pray in Jesus' name.

Praying in Christ's name means to pray in a manner consistent with His character and His life. And from the life of Jesus we find good examples for the kinds of requests we might include in our prayers.

For instance, I assumed that to pray for healing in His name would be answered by a repaired physical body. But God had a different kind of healing in mind—a spiritual healing.

We assume that it is God's will for us to have pure and polished reputations, but look at Jesus—He was slandered, mocked, and achieved national notoriety! We may be convinced that it is God's will for us to have a new and bigger house, but Jesus never had a real home or even a place to lay His head. We think words like *suffering* and *disappointment* shouldn't be included in the Christian's vocabulary, but Jesus was a man of sorrows, acquainted with grief.

Do you understand? When we pray in Jesus' name, we should expect to receive things consistent with that name: peace, patience, self-control, long-suffering, gentleness, sensitivity. We

---

> **"When we pray in Jesus' name, we should expect to receive things consistent with that name: peace, patience, self-control, long-suffering, gentleness, sensitivity."**

---

might pray for financial prosperity, a new career, success with the opposite sex, or physical healing, but God may choose to give us something even more precious, something even closer to what His name and character are all about.

His presence. His perspective. His endurance. His deep and lingering peace in the midst of turmoil and pain and loneliness and disappointment.

Will God give us health and a sterling reputation? Loyal friends? A new job? A mate? Perhaps. Then again, God may give you joy, just as He promised in John 16:24. With His joy, you can be complete, whatever the circumstances.

More About Praying in His Name

Take another look at John 16:23, " . . . my Father will give you whatever you ask in my name." When Jesus shared these words with His disciples, He was giving them a new perspective on how to have their needs met. He was teaching them how to seek. When we read, "my Father will give you," what more could we wish for than to have what God desires to give us? Remember, "No good thing does he withhold from those whose walk is blameless" (Psalm 84:11). And don't forget James 1:17: "Every good and perfect gift is from above, coming down from the Father of the heavenly lights."

When we ask "in His name," we ask for everything Christ purchased and promised through His death and resurrection. And to what has His death given us access? The Lord "has blessed us in the heavenly realms with every spiritual blessing in Christ" (Ephesians 1:3). When we pray in His name, we can be sure of this answer: God will bless us with every spiritual blessing. Now that's a big answer to prayer!

And look at John 16:24: "Until now you have not asked for anything in my name." Up until this point, His disciples had asked nothing in comparison to what was now ready to be poured out upon them. The Lord, by His death and resurrection, was ready to pour out His Spirit and give larger gifts than anyone realized. Perhaps the disciples had prayed before, but never had they prayed in the name of Christ and all that His name offered them.

"Ask and you will receive, and your joy will be complete" (John 16:24). Finally, when you think about it, isn't joy what you ultimately desire, whatever your petition? Whether you ask for yourself or on behalf of a friend, aren't you really looking for joy? Well, joy is promised. Joy is one of those spiritual blessings God is ready to pour out upon you. We are told to aim high in prayer, to expect to receive joy. Fullness of joy is ours as we pray without ceasing. "Be joyful always; pray continually" (1 Thessalonians 5:16–17).

And that is one answer to prayer that will always be a resounding "Yes!" Whatever your circumstances, God wants to give you joy. It's the highest and greatest result of praying in His name.

"When we pray in His name, we can be
sure of this answer: God will bless us
with every spiritual blessing.
Now that's a big answer to prayer!"

Prayer Point

When the Lord invited His followers to go to the Father in His name, He was talking about a brand-new relationship. Previously, men and women approached God with caution and fear through the priests. But since the resurrection of Jesus, all believers can talk to God personally . . . directly . . . anytime we want.

To get a clear idea of what it means to go to God "in Jesus' name," let's personalize, as a prayer, John 15. Say it with me now:

Jesus, You are the vine and our Father is the gardener. . . . I am already clean because of the word You have spoken to me. I remain in You and You remain in me because I, as the branch, can bear no fruit by myself; I must remain in You, the vine. . . . Apart from You, I can do nothing. As Your words remain in me and I remain in You, I may ask from You, and You will give to me so that You will receive glory. And this is Your glory—that I bear much fruit, showing myself to be Your disciple. In Your name, Amen.

What a way to pray—use Scripture and personalize it!

For Group Discussion

1. When have you prayed one way only to find God answered some other way?

2. Have you ever prayed for healing with sincere and certain faith but nothing happened? What answer do you think you really received?

3. How could suffering and disappointment be one way God answers prayer?

4. What does fullness of joy mean to you? When have you experienced pure joy? How is joy different from peace or happiness?

5. How can you pray in a way consistent with Jesus' character and life?

6. What does praying in Jesus' name really mean to you?

Part Three

Continuing On Through Praise

Thirteen

Seeking God with Praise

> Let praise—I say not merely thanksgiving, but
> praise—always form an ingredient of thy pray-
> ers. We thank God for what He is to us; for
> the benefits which He confers; and the bless-
> ings with which He visits us. But we praise
> Him for what He is in Himself, for His glori-
> ous excellences and perfections, independently
> of their bearing on the welfare of the creature.
>
> EDWARD M. GOULBURN

It's not often I casually flip through a book like Numbers, but the other day I came across an interesting story in chapter 21.

I read about the Israelites as they journeyed through the desert near the borders of Moab (Numbers 21:10ff.). Not a fun place, the desert. They were thirsty. The Israelites had one thought in their minds: *We need water, but we don't want snakes.* The last time they needed water they had complained against God, and God had sent venomous snakes in response (Numbers 21:5–9).

They had learned a painful lesson. This time they decided not to panic. No complaints. Instead, they praised. And God, in response, gave them water—a real miracle in a wilderness desert and a striking example of how God will refresh His saints when they praise Him.

I'm not unlike the Israelites—it's taken me awhile to learn that praise is the answer. There have been dry and dusty days in my soul, sometimes a coldness in my spirit. A cloud of gloom will hang heavily over me and no matter what I do or who I see, everything is an effort. At times like these, it's easy to complain.

As far as Satan is concerned, all this "makes his day." Satan claps his hands in glee when we wander in a dry and lifeless wilderness. One of his goals is to force complaints from the children of God and render useless our labor for the Lord. But there is a way out of that spiritual stalemate, and the answer is found in Numbers 21.

Praise the Lord. I don't mean that flippantly or superficially, and I'm not talking about a mechanical exercise either. I mean praise that is sincere, even if you have to grit your teeth and voice psalms of worship when your heart's not in it. Meaningful praise is sometimes praise you don't even feel. At least, not right away.

Even David the psalmist occasionally approached praise that way. You can almost hear him speak with a clenched jaw when he says in Psalm 57:7, "My heart is fixed, O God, my heart is fixed; I will sing and give praise" (KJV). You see, a fixed heart is a determined heart. David's heart was locked into trusting God and His sovereignty despite the difficulties.

You've been there before—the heavy sighing, the pain of even praying, let alone praising. You can take a giant step forward on your spiritual journey, straight out of the dry and barren desert, if you are able to say with the psalmist, "Why are you downcast, O my soul? Why so disturbed within me? Put your hope in God, for *I will yet praise him, my Savior and my God*" (Psalm 42:5, emphasis added).

Teach Us to Praise

Who, what, where, how, when, and *why.* Remember those words? Every time you opened your high school textbook to study, those words were your guide. If you could learn who did what, where, to whom, how, and why, you probably understood your subject.

It's no different when it comes to praising God. It's not something that comes naturally to any of us. Praise runs an aggravating interference pattern against our nature. It goes against our grain. Occasionally, praise feels more like a duty, an obligatory lip service performed at the opening of our prayers.

"Praising God . . . it's not something that comes naturally to any of us. Praise runs an aggravating interference pattern against our nature."

But remember David's words in Psalm 57:7, "My heart is fixed, O God, my heart is fixed; I will sing and give praise" (KJV). I like David's words, "I will." The psalmist refocused his emotions and realigned his thoughts by redirecting his will to praise. David taught himself that praise was good for his soul, as well as glorifying to God.

So *who* is to praise God? I am! You are! And not only us, but all of creation gets involved: "You will go out in joy and be led forth in peace; the mountains and hills will burst into song before you, and all the trees of the field will clap their hands" (Isaiah 55:12). And as someone has said, why should the trees have all the fun? Praise is befitting for God's people.

Where do we praise God? The psalms tell us to praise God "among the nations" and "among all peoples" (Psalm 96:3). Praise is fitting wherever we are—humming a praise song at the stoplight, quoting a favorite praise verse while you're folding laundry, repeating the words of a hymn of praise when you're gardening.

How do we praise God? With our mouths, with voices of joy, "with the psaltery," and with great shouts (Psalms 33:1–3; 63:5). The Bible says we can even praise God with "tambourine and dancing . . . with the strings and flute" (Psalm 150:4). I have a favorite album of instrumental music I've virtually memorized, and I love praising God in all the places where the melodies rise or the tunes become soft and gentle.

When do we do all this? Look at Psalm 34:1: "I will extol the LORD at all times." That's rather encompassing, isn't it? Other psalms tell us that we are to praise God all the day long, continually, or seven times a day (Psalms 35:28; 71:6; 119:164). I think one of the most meaningful times to praise God is when I wake up in the middle of the night and can't go back to sleep. It's comforting and reassuring to praise God "through the watches of the night" (Psalm 63:6).

Finally, *what* do we give praise for? Well, at least one psalm goes on for pages praising God for His mighty acts (Psalm 105). Elsewhere, we learn to praise God for His name, His Word, His mighty power, His wonders, and His faithfulness, to mention a few (Psalms 8:1; 56:4; 66:3; 89:5; 119:105). Perhaps Psalm 150:2 sums it up best: "Praise him for his surpassing greatness."

Why do we praise God? Romans 8:32 says it all: "He who did not spare his own Son, but gave him up for us all—how will he not also, along with him, graciously give us all things?" No wonder the heavenly choir sings, "Worthy is the Lamb, who was slain, to receive power and wealth and wisdom and strength and honor and glory and praise!" (Revelation 5:12). We praise God because He is worthy of our praise.

We Have No Reason to Fear God

Still, you may not consider yourself a good pupil of praise. If so, let me see if I can put my finger on the reason why: Of the

Trinity, whom do you relate to best? God the Father, Jesus the Son, or the Holy Spirit?

I know what you're thinking: *It's a trick question—they're all the same!* You're right, but I know many of us relate to the different Persons in the Trinity in very different ways.

I heard of a woman, for example, who was terrified of God the Father. She read all about Him in the Old Testament, how He commanded His leaders to destroy entire towns, how He slammed down an angry fist against sin, how He demanded a

---

"Maybe in the Old Testament people were afraid to approach God, but Jesus threw wide open the door of access to the Father, and that alone should cause us to praise."

---

high and holy standard. She couldn't relate to God the Father, much less praise Him.

But, she said, she could praise Jesus. She more easily related to Him. Jesus spent time reaching out to the hurting; He talked to handicapped people at the temple; He took a few minutes to chat with children; and He was always on the lookout for the underdog. Jesus was sensitive, kind, and compassionate—and this woman felt drawn to God the Son. She sensed no condemnation from Him, even when she stumbled and fell into sin. This woman prayed solely to Jesus—she opened all her conversations with God with the name of the Lord Jesus.

But then something amazing happened. She read the first chapter of Hebrews and learned that Jesus is the exact representation of God. She noticed a cross reference and flipped over to

John 1:18: "No one has ever seen God, but God the One and Only, who is at the Father's side, has made him known."

The woman was fascinated. She then realized that knowing Jesus was the same as knowing the Father. She had no reason to fear or tremble. She could relate to God the Father because He and the Son are one in the same.

Maybe in the Old Testament people were afraid to approach God, but Jesus threw wide open the door of access to the Father, and that alone should cause us to praise. What freedom. What confidence. We have no reason to fear and every reason to trust Him and give Him adoration and worship.

When We Can't Say Enough

Have you ever been so filled, so overflowing with praise that you could hardly stop? David had that happen: "My mouth is filled with your praise, declaring your splendor all day long" (Psalm 71:8). Have you ever been in a position where you simply can't say enough good things about God?

When I wrote my third book, *Choices . . . Changes,* a good chunk of chapters was devoted to my husband, Ken.

As I work on my books, sometimes I use my computer with my mouthstick, but most of the time I have to borrow other people's hands. One day my secretary sat next to me typing a mile a minute as I talked a mile a minute about Ken. I wrote about his muscles, and his smile, the way he stood, his muscles, how he dressed, the sparkle in his eyes, the gleam of his teeth, his muscles, the shine of his hair. After a while, my secretary said, "Joni, aren't you getting a little carried away? Haven't you said enough about Ken? I mean, that's the fourth time you've talked about his muscles." She was right.

But I love talking about Ken, and the words flowed effortlessly. You most likely talk like that about the ones you love, too. If you're a grandparent, you whip out those pictures of your grandkids. If you're enthralled in a romance, friends barely have to hint their interest and you're off and running at the mouth. You want others to know how proud you are of your kids, your grandchildren, your husband or wife, and your friends. Talking about the ones we love multiplies our pleasure.

The same was true for the writer of Hebrews. He couldn't say enough good things about his best Friend—Jesus. Look at the passage beginning in Hebrews 1:1:

> In the past God spoke to our forefathers through the prophets at many times and in various ways, but in these last days he has spoken to us by his Son, whom he appointed heir of all things, and through whom he made the universe. The Son is the radiance of God's glory and the exact representation of his being, sustaining all things by his powerful word. After he had provided purification for sins, he sat down at the right hand of the Majesty in heaven. So he became as much superior to the angels as the name he has inherited is superior to theirs.

Just glancing through this list gives us more than enough reasons to praise the Lord. Notice the seven "reasons to praise":

- Christ is the appointed heir of all creation. Right from the beginning, the writer lifts Jesus up to where He belongs.
- It was through the spoken word of Jesus that the universe was made. Look around you—everything from mountains to mulberry bushes was given life by the Lord Jesus.
- The Son is the radiance of God's glory. Just as the brilliance of the sun cannot be separated from the sun itself, Jesus can't be separated from the glory of the Father—He is God Himself.
- Jesus is the exact representation of the Father's being. Just as a stamp will leave its impression on warm wax, Jesus is the *exact* representation of the character and nature of God.
- Jesus is "sustaining all things by his powerful word" (1:3). Just as He created the world by the Word of His mouth, He is holding together all that has been created. What power!

- Jesus provided purification for sins—His wonderful work on the cross. By His death, Christ paid the huge penalty for our sins so that God's justice was satisfied.

- Jesus "sat down at the right hand of the Majesty in heaven" (1:3). His work of redemption completed, Jesus returned to His place by His Father's side. It is from His Father's throne that Jesus now rules over all.

The writer of Hebrews could have gone on and on talking about the One he loved the most. How is it with you? If someone asked you to list a few descriptive phrases about the Lord Jesus, would the words fall effortlessly from your mouth, or would you scramble for *Roget's Thesaurus*? If you find that you don't have enough adjectives to describe Him, spend a little time listening to the writer of Hebrews. You may find that before long you could write your own book about the Lord and you!

Prayer Point

Our mouths can be filled with His praises!

What has your mouth been full of so far today? Scolding? Nit-picking? Quibbling? Pause now and fix your heart on praise to God. Consider the who, where, why, and when of your praise. Speaking of when, why not right now?

If you have a thesaurus on your bookshelf (if not, a dictionary will do), look up words like *noble* and *great* and *honor* and then *praise*. Jot down synonyms so that you nearly fill an entire page. Now you have plenty of language to praise the Lord.

For Group Discussion

1. What might be a desert experience in a person's life?

2. What is genuine praise?

3. For what can you praise God?

4. What word best describes each person of the Trinity?

5. Brag about someone you love. Then do the same with Jesus.

6. What does this chapter teach you about praising God?

Fourteen

Seeking God Through Sacrifice

Let us continually offer to God a sacrifice of praise—the fruit of lips that confess his name.

HEBREWS 13:15

Neither will I offer burnt offerings unto the LORD my God of that which doth cost me nothing.

2 SAMUEL 24:24, KJV

S acrifice. Sound foreboding? A little off-putting?
To clear up the meaning of that word, my dictionary says that sacrifice is "a giving up of something valued for the sake of something else." When we sacrifice, it costs us, doesn't it?

That helps define for us "sacrifice of praise." But when do we ever praise God when it costs us something great?

If you praise the Lord through a minor hardship or a major trial, you are offering a sacrifice of praise. Such a sacrifice costs you plenty—your pride, your anger, your human logic, and the luxury of your complaining tongue. A sacrifice of praise costs you your will, your resentment, and even your desire to have your own way in a situation.

Whether it's a financial crunch, a sudden illness, or a personal defeat, if you fix your heart on praise to God, then you have offered a sacrifice. If you've ever cried during those heartbreaking difficulties, "Lord, I will hope in You and praise You more and more," then you know you have offered words which have cost you plenty. Praise in those circumstances is painful. Nevertheless, it is logical, even if our logic argues that God has no idea what He's doing.

Often, we assume that praise must be a bubbly explosion of enthusiastic phrases, happy and lighthearted words that tumble from an overflowing spirit. But that is not necessarily so. Psalm 65:1 describes a different kind of praise: "Praise awaits you, O God, in Zion; to you our vows will be fulfilled." I've been told that the Hebrew word for *awaiting* means "quiet trust." Those words don't sparkle with effervescence. It's like saying, "I have prayed about this burden, and now, Lord, I will quietly wait on You even before I see the answer. I expect it. And this is my sacrifice of praise to You—I believe and trust."

Please remember this: Most of the verses written about praise in God's Word were voiced by people who were faced with crushing heartaches, injustice, treachery, slander, and scores of other difficult situations. They knew that the sacrifice of praise was a key to victory on their spiritual journey.

Fixing My Heart on Praise

I remember a time when I was asked—almost forced—to present a sacrifice of praise to God. During the years when I was first in the hospital, I struggled to put together two sensible words in prayer to God. I would lie in bed and dream of the day the pain would go away. As well-intentioned as my nurses were, their starched white uniforms and name tags only added to the institutional feeling of that place. I hated my life.

I gave up on prayer. Praise? Far be it from me. I found solace in the luxury of a complaining tongue. I savored my anger, my resentment. I simply could not understand how a good God could allow something like my accident to happen to one of His children.

"If you praise the Lord through a minor hardship or a major trial, you are offering a sacrifice of praise. Such a sacrifice costs you plenty—your pride, your anger, your human logic, and the luxury of your complaining tongue."

My good friend, Steve Estes, began to set me straight. I liked this young Christian man because he always brought me Dunkin' Donuts or pizza or RC colas. So whenever he opened his Bible, I listened. Then came the day when he read 1 Thessalonians 5:18, "Give thanks in all circumstances, for this is God's will for you in Christ Jesus." He closed his Bible, looked at me and said gently, "Joni, it's about time you got around to giving thanks in that wheelchair of yours."

"Wait a minute. I can't do that," I said, a little shocked. "It wouldn't be spontaneous. I don't feel it, and I'm not going to be a hypocrite. I was enough of a hypocrite when I was in high school. I don't want to be a hypocrite anymore. I'm not going to give thanks when I don't feel like it."

Steve said, "Wait a minute, Joni, read the verse again. It doesn't say you've got to feel like a million bucks in everything. It says, 'Give thanks in all circumstances, for this is God's will for you in Christ Jesus.' Your thanks may not be spontaneous, but it can be a sacrifice. Trusting God's will is not necessarily having trusting feelings."

I argued, "I just can't thank God when I don't know why all this is happening."

Steve chided me gently. "Joni, even if the Lord were to tell you all the reasons why, it would be like pouring million-gallon truths into your one-ounce brain. God's ways are past finding out. You're just at the starting block of this long journey of life in a wheelchair. Don't expect to understand all the ins and outs from the very beginning."

"But I don't *feel* thankful," I whined.

"Well, the verse doesn't say 'feel thankful'—it says, 'give thanks.' There's a big difference."

So I gritted my teeth and, through tears, gave thanks. "Okay, Lord, I thank You for this hospital bed. I would really rather have the pizza and Dunkin' Donuts, but if You want me to have cafeteria oatmeal tomorrow, that's fine. And Lord, I thank You that physical therapy is benefiting me—thank You for all the flat-on-my-back ballet routine. Lord, I'm grateful that when I practiced writing the alphabet today with that pencil between my teeth, it didn't look like chicken scratch."

Some time later, I changed. Thankful feelings began to well up. It was as though God rewarded me with the feeling of gratitude for having obeyed and "given thanks."

And when I began to see that through giving thanks God was changing me and making me more like Jesus, it was no longer an effort to express gratitude. Perhaps in the beginning it had cost me my logic and my complaining, but praise came more easily after I saw the effects of such a sacrifice.

What Makes Praise Costly?

I can hear someone saying, "That's fine, Joni, but I'm not you. I handle problems differently. I put up with my hardships because they're my lot in life. I simply take a deep breath, and God and I charge ahead."

Now if I've described you, then you're the type who feels resigned to life. You may have a bit of the stoic in you, occasionally feeling like a martyr. But be honest—is resigning yourself to your problems really offering a sacrifice? I think you'll agree: Resignation is *not* a sacrifice of praise.

Then there are those folks who submit to their problems. They "ho" and they "hum" and sigh heavily. These dear people make certain everybody around sees they are bearing an impossible burden. But submission is not a sacrifice of praise either.

Well then, just what makes up a sacrifice of praise?

First, please don't think that you must be perfect in your praises to the Lord. Remember, He is not a rigid, unyielding God who forgets that "we are dust"; He "knows how we are formed" and remembers that we are only human (Psalms 103:14; 78:39). No matter how small or great the sacrifice, God knows the motive of your heart when you offer Him praise.

I learned that lesson in an odd way a few years ago.

You see, in the eighties, before the political changes in Poland, Ken and I visited that country where we spoke in churches and toured rehabilitation centers. When I returned to the States, I tried to share my impressions of Eastern Europe with a friend. I wanted to describe the warm and wonderful memory of being hugged by dear old Polish women who smelled faintly and sweetly of garlic. The hint of garlic was on their sweaters, coats, hands, even on their breath. Maybe before, garlic would have turned my nose, but since my visit, garlic became synonymous with laughter and smiles, happy embraces with new friends. Garlic meant . . . Poland.

But as I was about to describe this memory, I stopped short. You see, I don't think I could have explained that garlic equaled good things. To those of us in the West, garlic does not evoke the impression of a sweet, fragrant aroma. (Well, maybe it does if we're scarfing down our grandmother's famous lasagna.) For the most part, in this country the smell of garlic is about as pleasant as skunk spray.

One person's fragrance is another person's dread.

I occasionally think about that when I offer my sacrifices of praise to God. I want my offerings to be "a sweet-smelling aroma, an acceptable sacrifice, well pleasing to God" (Philippians 4:18, NKJV). I know what's on my heart as I wrench words of praise out of pain or hardship, and I believe God knows what's on my heart as well: "God, I'm hurting but You're my help . . . (long pause) . . . and I praise You . . . (brief moment of doubt, then a quick recovery) . . . and I will trust You . . . (am I sure? Yes, I am) . . . and rest in You . . . (another long pause) . . . in Jesus' name, Amen."

That may not sound like a sacrifice of praise to some, and if certain people were listening in, they'd think my sacrifice of praise smelled like garlic. They'd turn up their nose; they just wouldn't understand. But I know . . . God knows. And that's all that counts.

To summarize, when I think of a sacrifice of praise, I think of the word *embrace*. Embracing the will of God, even when the feelings aren't there, is offering to God your heart, wholly dedicated to His purpose. It is believing that, according to Romans 12, you can prove in practice that God's will for you is good and acceptable and perfect.

It'll cost—but oh, the worth of those words you offer your Lord.

A Living Sacrifice

I don't think we can talk about the sacrifice of praise without considering the bigger picture: our living sacrifice. We are to offer our bodies "as living sacrifices, holy and pleasing to God— this is your spiritual act of worship" (Romans 12:1).

A living sacrifice. I used to think of a bloody oblation on top of a brazen altar. Yuck. Well, that Old Testament image may not be all that different from what Paul meant in Romans 12. Frankly, when I read that verse I see myself on an altar. But this is where it changes—as soon as God strikes the match to light the flame of some fiery trial in my life, I imagine myself doing what any living sacrifice might do: I crawl off the altar!

This, to put it simply, is the dilemma Christians face. Living offerings have a way of creeping off the altar when the flames of a frustrating ordeal get a bit too hot. But the theme resounds through Scripture: He who loses his life for Christ's sake shall find it. Take up your cross—your altar of sacrifice—and follow Jesus. Since we died with Christ, we shall live with Him. If we die with Him, we shall reign with Him. There are scores of verses which sound the same theme.

"Living offerings have a way of creeping off the altar when the flames of a frustrating ordeal get a bit too hot."

As demanding as it may seem, God says that we are to present our bodies as living sacrifices, for this is our *reasonable* service. What's more, while we're on the altar, we're to praise God for the trial, because He is using it to mold us into the image of His Son. As our bodies are living sacrifices, our lips offer the sacrifice of praise. Sound reasonable?

Humanly speaking, no. With God's grace, yes.

Have you caught yourself crawling off the altar lately? Do you say you trust God with a certain problem and then sneak off the Lord's table to take things into your own hands? Or do you bargain with God from the altar, suggesting He turn down the flame a bit, as though He needed advice? Or do you argue with God about the length of time He's got you in the hot seat?

There's no getting around it. In view of God's mercies, in view of His single and great oblation for us, He asks of you and me the only kind of spiritual worship that is holy and pleasing to Him. A living offering you must be. Yes, you may squirm under the heat of the trial, but that doesn't change God's command. He's urging you today to get back up on the altar.

Let your life—your heart, your words, your body—be a sacrifice of praise to God.

Prayer Point

Pray as you sing this sacrifice of praise!

> Take my life and let it be
> Consecrated, Lord, to Thee;
> Take my moments and my days;
> Let them flow in ceaseless praise,
> Let them flow in ceaseless praise.
>
> Take my hands and let them move
> At the impulse of Thy love;
> Take my feet and let them be
> Swift and beautiful for Thee,
> Swift and beautiful for Thee.
>
> Take my will and make it Thine;
> It shall be no longer mine;
> Take my heart, it is Thine own;
> It shall be Thy royal throne,
> It shall be Thy royal throne.
>
> Take my love, my Lord, I pour
> At Thy feet its treasure store;
> Take myself and I will be
> Ever, only, all for Thee,
> Ever, only, all for Thee.

For Group Discussion

1. What is sacrificial about praising God when you don't feel like it?

2. How would you describe the difference between praising God out of joy and blessing and praising Him out of sorrow and pain?

3. What's the difference between praising God *in* a bad situation, and thanking Him *for* a bad situation?

4. How does praise help us get through difficult problems?

5. What bothers you about being a living sacrifice? What thoughts give you peace about it?

Fifteen

Seeking Victory Through Praise

O, do not pray for easy lives. Pray to be
stronger men. Do not pray for tasks equal to
your powers. Pray for powers equal to your
tasks.

PHILLIPS BROOKS,
Going Up to Jerusalem

D o you remember those high school chemistry days when
your class fooled around—excuse me, *experimented*—with
litmus paper? Remember, it was that little strip of paper that
you would place in certain liquids to see if they were acid or
alkaline. I can't remember what color the litmus paper turned if
you dipped it in acid—I think it was blue. And it turned red if
the substance was alkaline.

I thought it was rather amazing when, with a tight grip, I
would hold a piece of litmus paper, open my palm, and the
paper had turned red. A friend squeezed another piece of litmus, and his turned blue. Somebody else's litmus didn't turn
any color at all. We laughed at the guy who was the most acid of
us, telling him he was an old sourpuss.

The Marriage Litmus Test

Since I've married, I've realized that silly high school game with litmus paper can tell a lot about a person. Sometimes I think God intends my husband Ken to be, well, a big piece of litmus paper. And in marriage where two people can't help but be pressed up against one another, Ken has a way of revealing who I am and what I'm made of deep inside.

For instance, I hate those times when I'm mad as a hornet and he stays cool as a cucumber. That's when he's like a piece of litmus paper. His patience and love only show up my own love-lessness and selfishness. The more love he demonstrates, the more ugly I feel in my own anger. I'm an old sourpuss up against him.

To be fair, there are plenty of moments when he is upset over some silliness and God gives me the grace to demonstrate love. That's when I'm like a piece of litmus paper to Ken. The sweeter I am, the more convicted he becomes.

Not long ago Ken and I had one of those "litmus test" quarrels. I found him using my good eyebrow tweezers to pick fleas off Scruffy, our dog. I couldn't believe it. He didn't even ask—he just rummaged around in my bathroom drawer, pulled out my tweezers, and proceeded to pick fleas off the dog. Then he didn't even wipe the tweezers with Lysol. He just dropped them back in my drawer.

I was outraged! "What in the world are you doing?"

That was all it took for him to remind me that I ought to tell the girls who get me up in the morning to quit using his razors to shave my underarms!

Before you know it, we were quarreling hot and heavy. The words flew back and forth, and after half an hour, Ken slammed the door on me in the bedroom. I was fuming, so I decided I would enjoy the tactical satisfaction of turning my wheelchair to the sliding glass door to stare out at the backyard. When he returned to the bedroom, he'd find me there and feel bad.

Twenty minutes went by, and finally Ken walked back in. He sighed, sat on the edge of the bed, and shook his head. We sat there in stubborn silence.

Finally I spoke up. "I'm sorry, Ken. I don't like you."

He thought and then retorted, "I don't like you either."

"What are we going to do?" I asked.

"I don't know." Another long moment passed. "I guess we ought to pray."

"Okay, you start."

"I resented the effort my husband was making. The more he talked about how great God was, the more loveless I felt."

My eyes were shooting such pointed darts, I don't know how Ken could pray, but he clasped his fingers tightly and began mouthing well-worn phrases. His voice faltered and he stumbled with his words. He spoke about the goodness and greatness of the Lord, yet I knew his heart wasn't in it.

I resented the effort my husband was making. The more he talked about how great God was, the more loveless I felt. It was as though Ken's words were a piece of litmus paper. God was pressing his prayer up against me, and my pH balance looked sour, so full of acid.

I tried to close my ears to Ken's words of praise. Even though his prayer wasn't spontaneous, it was genuine. Conviction grew in me. Mysteriously, Ken's words became softer, and I began to hear his heart break in his prayer. Tears came to my eyes, and my anger dissipated—it was all I could do to keep from stopping Ken from praying so I could tell him how much I loved him.

I had never seen anything so beautiful as my husband sitting there praising God. He looked up with tears in his eyes and said, "Your turn."

I was numb. Finally I stammered, "Ken, I feel awful. I just need to confess to God how rotten I am. I can't believe I made such a big deal over a pair of eyebrow tweezers."

I bowed my heart before the Lord, and next thing I knew, my husband and I were singing praises to God together. After a few moments, Ken said, "Joni, I feel like a burden has just been lifted off my shoulders."

I looked at my watch. "Did that feeling happen just five seconds ago?"

"Yes, it did."

"I don't believe it. That's exactly when I felt the same heavy load lift off me." We embraced one another. It was his praise that turned this emotionally troublesome time into a victory. A litmus test and praise had brought us closer together—and God gave us the victory over Satan.

Praise Is Our Best Weapon

Praising God was the last thing on our mind that day we quarreled. But your spouse is not your enemy, nor are your circumstances. Your children aren't the enemy, and neither is your boss at work. We wrestle not against the flesh and blood of daily problems—our enemy is Satan. Our battle is with him.

If you think you have it tough, consider the story of Paul and Silas told in Acts 16. These two preachers were falsely accused by the owners of a slave girl who had been freed from a demon. Upset that their means of financial support was now gone, they accused Paul and Silas of throwing the city into an uproar.

The magistrates ordered Paul and Silas to be stripped and beaten. After being flogged, they were put in chains and thrown into prison. The jailer placed them in the innermost dungeon and guarded them carefully.

Imagine their pain—their wounds were caked with dried blood; welts and bruises covered their backs; and the damp prison air went right through them. Perhaps Paul felt faint or Silas was sick to his stomach.

"Your spouse is not your enemy, nor are your circumstances. Your children aren't the enemy, and neither is your boss at work. We wrestle not against the flesh and blood of daily problems—our enemy is Satan. Our battle is with him."

Who would have blamed them for whining or complaining? But Paul and Silas directed their thoughts toward God, not their accusers. They chose to pray and sing hymns loud enough for the other prisoners to hear—in other words, they triumphed in their praise.

Even though men and Satan attacked them, Paul and Silas won the battle *with their words*. Perhaps Paul and Silas even called on Psalm 106:47, "Save us, O LORD our God, and gather us from among the heathen, to give thanks unto thy holy name, and to triumph in thy praise" (KJV).

Once again, victory came as a result of praise.

Weapons from Our Mouths

Words of praise. Do we really understand their power?

Do we grasp the mighty force behind the things we say? Do we recognize the dynamics behind the sentences we speak to each other? The things we say before God? Before the devil? No wonder the tongue is given so much attention in the book of James!

I had a friend whose life was a story of praise and victory. Denise was my roommate for almost two years when I was in the hospital. She was blind and paralyzed, a beautiful seventeen-year-old black high school girl from Baltimore. I had the advantage of being able to sit up in a wheelchair once in a while, but Denise remained in bed.

I'll never forget the praise my friend was able to offer. This might sound a little other-worldly, but sometimes I wonder if our hospital room wasn't cleared of demons and evil powers simply because of her praise. And I wonder if God began His work of emotional redemption in my life through Denise, who, blind and paralyzed, paved the way, gaining the victory over the devil in our room.

In Ephesians 3:10 we read, "His intent was that now, through the church, the manifold wisdom of God should be made known to the rulers and authorities in the heavenly realms." In other words, Denise, lying in her bed, may not have been much of a testimony to the busy doctors and nurses or to occasional friends who dropped by, but her praise to God reached far beyond that hospital room to touch the heavenlies.

Denise, in praising the Lord, was winning a battle that you and I only glimpse now and then. She was living on a higher plane, a dimension that I wasn't sure even existed. Denise's life was the battleground upon which the mightiest forces of the universe converged in warfare. And she gained the victory through her praise to God.

Our Watchful Witnesses

You and I are hardly in Denise's condition. In fact, unlike Denise, you may rub shoulders with scores of people every day. Your testimony is seen by hundreds of people in a week—the bag boy at the local supermarket, the gas station attendant who fills your tank, the woman at the dry cleaners, your neighbor, the people at PTA, your friends at choir rehearsal. You meet people every day. Do they see in you a life devoted to godly praise?

And even if you're living alone in a small apartment, hardly interacting with anyone, your commitment to praise God counts. For there are a great many "somebodies" watching you. God

---

"When you bite your tongue from the luxury of complaining, you are gaining victory against the devil. When you praise God, you are showing the heavenly hosts, powers, and principalities, the demons of darkness, and the angels of light that your great God is worthy of praise—no matter what your circumstances."

---

uses your praise as a witness to angels and demons about His wisdom and power.

When you bite your tongue from the luxury of complaining, you are gaining victory against the devil. When you praise God, you are showing the heavenly hosts, powers, and principalities, the demons of darkness, and the angels of light that your great God is worthy of praise—no matter what your circumstances.

Our words of praise reach farther than we can imagine. Victory is found in praise.

Prayer Point

Has it ever struck you that your prayers are a testimony to the heavenly hosts? Amazing, isn't it?

The next time you're tempted to think that your response to your trials isn't doing anybody any good, before you give up the battle, turn to Ephesians 3:10. It might help to remind you that somebody's watching—and you might even find yourself listening for the rustling of wings.

In fact, why don't you read Ephesians 3:10 right now:

> His intent was that now, through the church, the manifold wisdom of God should be made known to the rulers and authorities in the heavenly realms.

Spend a few moments in praise to God, mindful that others are listening!

For Group Discussion

1. Think of a friend who has a close relationship with God. What have you noted or learned about prayer from that person?

2. When would it be appropriate to praise God in the middle of a conflict, and when would it be inappropriate?

3. In what ways is praise like a weapon? Against whom is the weapon to be used?

4. How does praise help us succeed in living the Christian life?

5. What's the relationship between praise and confession?

6. For what can you praise God right now?

Sixteen

Seeking Confidence In Life's Challenges

> I have been driven many times to my knees by
> the overwhelming conviction that I had no-
> where else to go.
>
> ABRAHAM LINCOLN

When I was on my feet, I loved horseback riding. I used to train horses to jump and would often enter them in horse shows around Maryland and Pennsylvania. I'd polish my boots, soap my saddle, and starch and iron my shirt. I worked hard, but nowhere near as hard as my thoroughbred, Auggie.

My horse was one of those tall, thin thoroughbreds with long legs. He looked like an adolescent who hadn't grown into his feet yet. Auggie didn't have the best conformation, but those legs carried us over some of the highest and broadest fences. And in the show ring, he was absolutely trusting and obedient to me.

When we would approach the first fence, I'd simply tighten my knees against the saddle, and off he would go in a flash. He'd confidently canter toward the fence; I'd angle his head, and he'd fly swiftly over it. I'd rein his head toward the next fence, and he'd leap over that one, hurdling a complex maze of jumps.

Maneuvering a horse through a confusing series of difficult hurdles requires a trusting and obedient horse. The horse has to trust that the rider knows what he's doing—I had knowledge of what lay ahead in the course and Auggie didn't. Trusting and obeying. Leading and guiding. Auggie and I had that kind of relationship.

Are You Facing Hurdles?

For us humans, the path of life before us often seems like an incredibly complex maze of hurdles we're expected to cross over. Have you ever felt like you were on a track, running with all your might and not knowing what was to come next? We can't see over the hurdle, and because it's so high, we're not sure we want to even go on to the next one. We feel like disobeying. We feel like running out on the course of life.

But listen. Auggie's trusting response did not hinge on his approval of the course. My horse didn't understand jumps. He had no idea about the degree of difficulty. All he knew was me.

I wish I were more like my horse! Isaiah 1:3 says, "The ox knows his master, the donkey his owner's manger, but Israel does not know, my people do not understand." Why is it we cannot, do not, trust God? Maybe we just don't know who God is, or how much He has done for us.

Look at Paul's confidence in the Lord. In Scripture we never hear Paul say, "I understand why these things are happening, Lord, and so I'll offer you praise." No. His praise was often a sacrifice because he *didn't* know what was around the next bend. Nevertheless, Paul trusted and obeyed. He didn't know why things were happening, what was ahead, or how difficult it would be, but he knew in Whom he believed: "Yet I am not ashamed, because I know whom I have believed, and am convinced that he is able to guard what I have entrusted to him for that day" (2 Timothy 1:12).

For Paul, the supreme reason he could praise his Lord was simply this: he knew his Lord. The apostle was able to praise his Lord because Jesus had bought his trust at the Cross.

When You Can't See over the Hurdle

Nothing beats good advice. A man named Ted Smith wrote me a few years ago and offered this: "Many believers gaze at their problems and glance at the Lord. But I tell you to gaze at the Lord and glance at your problems."

"Too many of us fix our eyes on our problems—the hurdles—and we start measuring the height of the next jump. In so doing, we glance occasionally at the Lord only to make sure He's aware of all the hardships."

Great advice! Too many of us fix our eyes on our problems—the hurdles—and we start measuring the height of the next jump. In so doing, we glance occasionally at the Lord only to make sure He's aware of all the hardships these hurdles are causing us.

Trouble is, the course God has set before us seems so . . . difficult! The dog has tracked Alpo all over the kitchen floor. Your husband has called to say he'll be late. The saucepans are boiling over, and the burning casserole is staining your oven. Teenagers are wrestling in the bedroom above your kitchen. Little wonder you stand there with the dish towel in your hand, droop-shouldered and dumbfounded, not knowing what to do.

You mutter an obligatory prayer as you tramp upstairs to referee the latest family argument. Sound familiar? You sigh in frustration as God barely gets noticed in all the hoopla.

What we need here is more than a prayer mumbled in obligation. We need the attitude of Abraham Lincoln when he said, "I have been driven many times to my knees by the overwhelming conviction that I had nowhere else to go." We need a different focus.

Consider Hebrews 12:2–3: "Let us fix our eyes on Jesus, the author and perfecter of our faith, who for the joy set before him endured the cross, scorning its shame, and sat down at the right hand of the throne of God. Consider him who endured such opposition from sinful men, so that you will not grow weary and lose heart."

It really is a matter of focus, isn't it? Consider Jesus. He had one heavy cross to bear, but He fixed His sight on the joy before Him. And we are to do the same.

So what about the burning casserole, the dirty kitchen floor, and the screaming kids upstairs? They haven't changed. But your focus has. Don't gaze at your problems while you only glance at the Lord. Get life in focus. Gaze at the Lord—behold Him—and your problems won't cause you to grow weary and lose heart.

Earning the Prize

Auggie, my wonderful horse, taught me a lot about why I ought to praise God. After the course in the show ring was completed, and he was hot and lathered, I'd jump down and lead him out to the paddock. Often the judges called us back into the ring. As we stood in front of the judges' box, Auggie would shake his head and stamp his feet impatiently until a person of great importance walked up to him—and handed me the trophy. Auggie did all the work, but I received the honors.

Do you see the parallel? You and I are in training to trust and obey. This whole adventure we're on is a growing relation-

---

"You and I are in training to trust and obey. This whole adventure we're on is a growing relationship of trust and obedience between us and the One who is holding the reins in our life."

---

ship of trust and obedience between us and the One who is holding the reins in our life. While we are leaping through our complex maze of hurdles in this pattern of life, the eyes of the Judge are upon us. And on the day of completion, when we have been "trained" in godliness, the Lord Jesus will walk up to us and award us a prize. What an honor!

The Bible makes it clear that you and I are to be for the praise of Christ's glory. Consider these verses from Ephesians:

> He predestined us to be adopted as his sons through Jesus Christ, in accordance with his pleasure and will. . . . In him we were also chosen, having been predestined according to the plan of him who works out everything in conformity with the purpose of his will. . . . I pray also that the eyes of your heart may be enlightened in order that you may know the hope to which he has called you, the riches of his glorious inheritance in the saints. (Ephesians 1:5, 11, 18)

Do you see? We receive the inheritance of Christ so that we may bring Him glory! All the praise goes to the Lord Jesus. Sure, we do much of the work here on earth—there's a lot of training and preparation. The course is long and complex, and at times we get weary and wonder if it's really worth it all. But every moment the eyes of the Judge are upon us. He sees our successes and our failures. For all our efforts, for all the times we obey, Jesus will receive the glory.

As you go about your duties today, remember what—remember who—your work is for. It is to be for the praise of His glory. The more you obey, the greater the honor He receives.

Jesus gets the glory—there's no better reason to praise Him.

Prayer Point

Try sharpening your focus right now. Spend a little time thinking about Hebrews 12:2–3:

> Let us fix our eyes on Jesus, the author and perfecter of our faith, who for the joy set before him endured the cross, scorning its shame, and sat down at the right hand of the throne of God. Consider him who endured such opposition from sinful men, so that you will not grow weary and lose heart.

Perhaps you can write this out and tape it above your kitchen sink, on the dash of your car, or above your desk. That way, life will stay in focus.

Something that helps me keep my life in focus is the doxology, the church's anthem of victorious praise. If you know the tune, sing it now:

> Praise God from Whom all blessings flow,
> Praise Him, all creatures here below.
> Praise Him above, ye heavenly hosts,
> Praise Father, Son, and Holy Ghost.

Keep this in mind next time you're facing life's challenges!

For Group Discussion

1. What was one of your favorite childhood activities that you worked or practiced hard at (soccer, piano, dance,

raising an animal, chess, swimming, etc.)? What insights, if any, does this give you into prayer?

2. When have you faced a hurdle in life that you couldn't see over?

3. What is often the worst time of your day or week? What could you do to focus on Christ at that time—gaze instead of glance at Him—that would help you get through it?

4. What are the biggest everyday hurdles you face? How can you focus your thoughts on Jesus as you approach them?

5. What can you do to change your focus?

Seventeen

Seeking God's Glory Through Prayer and Praise

> Prayer crowns God with the honor and glory
> due to His name, and God crowns prayer with
> assurance and comfort.
>
> THOMAS BENTON BROOKS

D o you ever feel like you and God are a team, but you're doing all the work? Do you resent that? Perhaps that's why, when you think of heavenly crowns, you see yourself holding your crown a little too tightly, unwilling to lay it at the feet of Jesus (Revelation 4:10).

In case you're confused about who deserves the honors, read the following. You'll be reminded of how thankful we ought to be that God gives us the opportunity to earn honors for Him:

> Jesus Christ deserved glory, but He was humbled.
> He deserved love, but He was hated by many.
> He deserved worship, but many rejected Him.
> He deserved praise, but often He was mocked
>   and scorned.
> He deserved comfort, but He didn't have a home.
> He deserved riches, but He lived in poverty.
> He deserved holiness, but He became sin for us.

In spite of all these things, Jesus never got confused about whom to honor. He never lost His praise to God. He had reasons to offer gratefulness to the Father, and He never ceased to give prayerful appreciation. He never lost sight of the joy set before Him.

But in contrast, look at us:

> We deserve humility, but we receive glory.
> We deserve rejection, but God gives us sonship.
> We deserve judgment, but we receive mercy.
> We are worthy of poverty, but He chooses to give
> us riches and make us part of the inheritance
> of the Son.
> We ought to be charged with sin's curse,
> but instead He gives us righteousness.

That, if anything, should clear up any confusion we have about who deserves the honors, who deserves the praise. And prayer is the best forum from which to give Christ His just glory. Look at the prayers Paul offered when he wrote even the first few lines of his epistles—whether Colossians 1 or Ephesians 1, Paul started out giving praise to God. Perhaps it was because he knew what he deserved—hell—and that made him give to God all the more ceaseless and heartfelt praise.

A Sweet Reminder of Jesus

When we "get it straight" about who gets the praise, we bring delight to God. Can you imagine? You and I can actually move the heart of the Lord of the universe. Just read these verses and imagine the smile of God: "Here is my servant, whom I uphold, my chosen one in whom I delight" (Isaiah 42:1). And also, "The LORD will take delight in you. . . . As a bridegroom rejoices over his bride, so will your God rejoice over you" (Isaiah 62:4–5).

What a privilege it is to bring God joy! The following will help illustrate what I mean.

I love crisp, cold days when you can smell the smoke of a cherry-wood fire from a neighbor's chimney. Or you can stick your head out the back bedroom window, draw a deep breath, and almost taste the scent of pine from the little woods on the other side of the fence. I love the smell of fresh, damp laundry that you hang outside on the line.

"Your prayers, like all acts of service, rise like a sweet-smelling savor, a fragrant sacrifice that pleases God (Philippians 4:18). And that fragrance of your prayers is a reminder to the Father of the sweet-smelling sacrifice of the life of His Son."

In fact, to this day, smelling Tide laundry detergent brings back vivid memories of my father's T-shirts and good times helping my mom fold sweet-smelling towels. Fragrances bring beautiful memories to mind. I'm sure that's why the perfume industry is a multimillion-dollar business. Perfume experts know a whiff of English Leather or a sniff of Chanel No. 5 can make us recall crystal clear, wonderful remembrances.

However, God's Word knew the power of perfume long before the chemists at Revlon. In 2 Corinthians 2:14 Paul wrote, "But thanks be to God, who always leads us in triumphal procession in Christ and through us spreads everywhere the fragrance of the knowledge of him."

That idea was borrowed from the ancient Roman parades of triumph. The apostle Paul compared himself, first, to one of the prisoners led in long chains behind the conqueror's chariot;

then, to a servant bearing incense; and lastly, to the incense itself that rose all along the procession of triumph.

Paul knew the power behind a sweet fragrance. It is as though he were saying, "I desire to live that I may perpetually remind God of the obedience, sacrifice, and devotion of the Lord Jesus. I want my words and deeds to bring to the mind of God those wonderful, similar memories of the earthly life of Jesus."

Isn't that a glorious thought? Your prayers, like all acts of service, rise like a sweet-smelling savor, a fragrant sacrifice that pleases God (Philippians 4:18). And that fragrance of your prayers is a reminder to the Father of the sweet-smelling sacrifice of the life of His Son (Ephesians 5:2). Your prayers make God smile.

Who Else Brings God Joy?

Sometimes I like to think that my prayers of praise are like one or two small drops in a vast ocean of joyful adorations that have gone up before God for countless ages. In other words, our lives of prayer aren't the only lives that touch the heart of God.

A few years ago when Ken and I traveled to Europe, the highlight of the trip was when we attended a service at St. Paul's Cathedral in London. We arrived on a Sunday afternoon in time for the late service. As we sat there in the hush of the cool cathedral, I was carried away by the echo of church bells above me.

The few of us gathered for the service bowed our heads in quiet respect as we prayed in this sanctuary where thousands of saints had worshiped for centuries. As in days of old, the candles warmed the cathedral with a soft glow, reflecting off the faces of the boys in the choir. The choir chanted Gregorian canticles, an old and familiar harmony that has reached the rafters of that grand cathedral for hundreds of years.

In St. Paul's Cathedral people prayed for safety during the sweep of the Black Plague. And George Whitefield prayed for the souls of the men to whom he preached. Perhaps David Liv-

ingstone prayed there before embarking on his missionary jour-
neys. Kings and queens of Europe bowed their knees in prayer
in St. Paul's; dignitaries and statesmen, too. And maybe the Pil-
grims and settlers who sailed from England to America had
friends who prayed for their safety from under the arches where
I was sitting.

**"You have an open invitation to enter
the heart of God through prayer and
praise today. Prayer is your point of
contact with the Lord of the universe."**

As I stared at the high gilded ceiling, the heavy tapestries,
and the carved marble statues, I was reminded of Hebrews 12:1:
"Therefore, since we are surrounded by such a great cloud of
witnesses, let us throw off everything that hinders and the sin
that so easily entangles, and let us run with perseverance the
race marked out for us."

As I wheeled away after the service, I thought of all the
praying Christians who now sit in the grandstands of heaven.
They have set an example, and God has used their prayers to
protect His Word, advance His gospel, strengthen His church,
and teach us today of the power of praise and prayer.

But "grandstand people" don't have to be saints of old.
These heroes of the faith can be our neighbors, our pastors—
even you can be a spiritual hero. You can be a grandstand person to someone else who is waiting to see another Christian per-
severe in prayer, take seriously the call to intercede, and believe
mightily that praise has power.

To God Be the Glory

Picture yourself now at that great Day yet to happen. "For we must all appear before the judgment seat of Christ, that each one may receive what is due him for the things done while in the body, whether good or bad" (2 Corinthians 5:10).

It is your turn. Jesus looks through the books, smiles at you and says, "Well done, good and faithful servant! You have been faithful with a few things; I will put you in charge of many things" (Matthew 25:21). He hands you a crown. Perhaps a few crowns: The crown that will last (1 Corinthians 9:25–27), the crown of rejoicing (1 Thessalonians 2:19–20), the crown of righteousness (2 Timothy 4:8), the crown of life (James 1:12), and the crown of glory (1 Peter 5:2–4).

You feel the heavy diadem; you hold it and run your fingers over it. You can't believe the crown is really in your hands. As you stand there, other saints gather around and kneel before the King of kings to lay their crowns at His feet (Revelation 4:4,10). What do you see yourself doing—tightly clutching your crown, or falling to your knees and presenting it with tears of joy to your great God and Savior?

That Day is coming soon. Why wait until eternity to know the Lord intimately? Why delay until the judgment seat of Christ to offer Him praise? You have an open invitation to enter the heart of God through prayer and praise today. Prayer is your point of contact with the Lord of the universe. Prayer is an investment in heavenly glories above—much like those crowns.

Prayer is seeking God. And it's your personal journey. No one else can do your work of prayer, intercede for the people you know, offer God praises that are unique and special . . . no one can do this labor of love but you.

Prayer and praise—it's your journey. And as you step out into it, you'll discover the journey is wonderful because you have sought and found God.

Prayer Point

Always remember, you have the opportunity to communicate intimately and personally with the Son of God through prayer. But praying, just like any communication, is something you want to do with someone you know. If you don't know the Lord Jesus, you can meet Him right now with a very simple prayer like this one:

Dear Lord Jesus, I realize my life has been far from You, and I know that sin has been the barrier between us. Please come into my heart and mind and spirit, and Father, through Your forgiveness, make me the person You want me to be. Forgive me for turning away from You. Give me the power to follow You as I invite You to be the Lord of my life. Thank You for the difference You will make because of the Lord Jesus. Amen.

For Group Discussion

1. When have you felt cheated out of recognition or honor that you thought you deserved?

2. When have you received recognition or honor that you really didn't deserve?

3. Who in your life brings you joy? Why? What have you done that you believe has brought joy to God?

4. In your Christian walk so far, what's one worship experience that stands out? Where was it and why was it memorable?

5. When you think of someone "watching you from the grandstands," who comes to mind (both living and dead)? How does this motivate you?

6. Imagine finally seeing God face-to-face. What is the first thing that you would like to say or do? How can you do that now?

7. How has this book helped you in your journey of prayer and praise?

In Closing . . .

L ike you, I'm still progressing in my journey of seeking God through prayer and praise. Sometimes on the journey I get diverted, take a side trail, or occasionally even forget where I'm going. But not long ago I reached a kind of milestone—I'm praying more and enjoying it more! And I'm discovering that prayer is the way into the heart of the Lord Jesus.

Part of this discovery is due to several books I've devoured, reading and rereading them until the author's message got through. *Love On Its Knees* and *The Hour That Changes the World* by Dick Eastman (Baker Book House) have springboarded me into the lively work of global intercession. I have enjoyed praying for disabled people in countries around the world! I highly recommend these two books if you are interested in taking a giant step forward in your journey.

And since you're a fellow journeyman, I would love to hear from you. At *Joni and Friends* we have a prayer team of over four hundred people who intercede on behalf of the many people with disabilities and their families whom we touch for Christ. If you would like to join this prayer team, please let me know!

JONI AND FRIENDS
P.O. Box 3333
Agoura Hills, CA 91301
(818) 707–5664
TDD: (818) 707–7006

About the Author

Although a diving accident in 1967 left Joni a quadriplegic in a wheelchair, her limitations have not slowed her down. Joni is not only an internationally-known mouth artist, but her first name is recognized in many countries of the world due to her best-selling books, including her autobiography, *Joni*.

During the nearly twenty-five years of her paralysis, Joni has learned to rely on help from friends and grace from God. Her severe disability has drawn her into a deeper study of God's Word and a rich insight into praise and intercession—all of which is poignantly revealed in the pages of *Seeking God*.

Joni and her husband, Ken, a high school history teacher, reside in Woodland Hills, California. They play chess, follow NCAA tournaments, go camping in the Sierras, and enjoy their miniature schnauzer, Scruffy.

The typeface for the text of this book is *Caledonia* which was created by the talented type and book designer, William Addison Dwiggins. Dwiggins, who became acting director of the Harvard University Press in 1917, was also known for his work with the publisher Alfred Knopf and for his other type designs, notably *Electra*. The name *Caledonia* is the ancient name for what is now the country of Scotland and denotes that the type was originally designed to parallel *Scotch Roman* (sometimes described as a *Modernized Old Style*). In creating *Caledonia*, Dwiggins was also influenced by the type that William Martin cut in 1790 for William Bulmer. Thus *Caledonia* is a modification of *Bulmer* and *Scotch Roman*, yet it is more business-like and versatile than the two older types.

Substantive Editing:
Michael S. Hyatt

Copy Editing:
Angela Elwood Hunt

Cover Design:
Steve Diggs & Friends
Nashville, Tennessee

Page Composition:
Xerox Ventura Publisher
Linotronic L-100 Postscript® Imagesetter

Printing and Binding:
Maple-Vail Book Manufacturing Group
York, Pennsylvania

Dust Jacket Printing:
Strine Printing Company
York, Pennsylvania